HOME AND BEAUTY

A Farce in Three Acts

by

W. SOMERSET MAUGHAM

SAMUEL FRENCH

LONDON
NEW YORK   TORONTO   SYDNEY   HOLLYWOOD

HOME AND BEAUTY

Produced at The Arts Theatre, London, on Thursday, August 31st, 1950, and transferred to St Martin's Theatre, London, on Wednesday, September 27th, 1950, with the following cast of characters:

(in the order of their appearance)

VICTORIA (*a dear little thing*)	Brenda Bruce
MISS DENNIS (*a manicurist*)	Marjorie Dunkels
TAYLOR (*the maid*)	Virginia Hewit
MRS SHUTTLEWORTH (VICTORIA's *mother*)	Susan Richmond
LEICESTER PATON (*a wangler*)	John Boxer
MAJOR FREDERICK LOWNDES, D.S.O. (*a hero*)	Anthony Marlowe
MAJOR WILLIAM CARDEW, D.S.O. (*another hero*)	Hugh Burden
NANNIE (*the nurse*)	Peggy Ann Clifford
MRS POGSON (*a cook*)	May Hallatt
A. B. RAHAM (*a solicitor*)	Brian Oulton
MISS MONTMORENCY (*a maiden lady*)	Barbara Leake
CLARENCE (*an errand boy*)	Trevor Hill

SYNOPSIS OF SCENES

The action of the play passes in VICTORIA's house at Westminster, London, during 1919.

ACT I. VICTORIA's bedroom. Afternoon.

ACT II. The drawing-room. The following morning.

ACT III. The kitchen. Noon, the next day.

HOME AND BEAUTY

ACT I

SCENE.—VICTORIA's *bedroom in her house at Westminster, London. An afternoon in 1919.*

It is the kind of bedroom which is used only to sleep in, but might just as well be a sitting-room. Through an arch up C. *there is an alcove with the only door to the room* R. *of it. There is a window down* R. *and a fireplace down* L. *The furniture is graceful; attractive pictures hang on the walls; there are vases of flowers and it is all very comfortable, luxurious and modish. The bed with its hangings and its beautiful coverlet stands in an alcove* R., *above the window. A great lacquer dressing-table, crowded with the necessary aids to feminine beauty, stands under the window, with a chair in front of it. There is a long stool at the foot of the bed. A console table stands against the back wall of the alcove up* C. *There is a washstand against the back wall* L. *of the alcove. There is a small sofa* L.C. *with a stool* L. *of it and a small table* R. *of it. A comfortable armchair stands* C. *The floor is carpeted and at night the room is lit by electric-candle wall-brackets over the mantelpiece and a pendant light over the bed. A bright fire burns in the grate.*

(*See the Ground Plan at the end of the Play.*)

When the CURTAIN *rises* VICTORIA *is lying on the sofa having her hands manicured by* MISS DENNIS *who is seated on the stool* L. *of the sofa.* VICTORIA *is a pretty little thing and wears a lovely "confection" which is partly tea-gown and partly dressing-gown.* MISS DENNIS, *the manicurist, is a neat, trim person of twenty-five. She has a slight Cockney accent.*

MISS DENNIS (*evidently just ending a long story*). And so at last I said to him, "Oh, very well, 'ave it your own way."

VICTORIA. One has to in the end, you know.

MISS DENNIS. He's asked me five times, and I really got tired of saying "no". And then, you see, in my business you get to know all the ins and outs of married life, and my impression is that, in the long run, it don't really matter very much who you marry.

VICTORIA. Oh, I do so agree with you there. It all depends on yourself. When my first husband was killed, poor darling, I went all to pieces. My bust simply went to nothing. I couldn't wear a low dress for months.

MISS DENNIS. How dreadful.

VICTORIA. I simply adored him. But you know, I'm just as fond of my second husband.

Miss Dennis. You must have one of those loving natures.

Victoria. Of course, I should never survive it if anything happened to my present husband, but if anything did—touch wood—you know, I couldn't help myself, I'd just have to marry again, and I know I'd love my third husband just as much as I loved the other two.

Miss Dennis (*sighing*). Love is a wonderful thing.

Victoria. Oh, wonderful. Of course, I'd wait the year. I waited the year when my first was killed.

Miss Dennis. Oh yes, I think one always ought to wait the year.

Victoria. I noticed you had an engagement ring on the moment you came in.

Miss Dennis. I didn't really ought to wear it during business hours, but I like to feel it's there.

Victoria. I know the feeling so well. You turn it round under your glove, and you say to yourself, "Well, that's settled." Is he nice looking?

Miss Dennis. Well, he's not what you might call exactly handsome, but he's got a nice face.

Victoria. Both my husbands have been very handsome men. You know, people say it doesn't matter what a man looks like, but that's all nonsense. There's nothing shows a woman off like a good-looking man.

Miss Dennis. He's very fair.

Victoria. Of course, it's all a matter of taste, but I don't think I should like that myself. They always say fair men are deceitful. Both my husbands were dark, and they both had the D.S.O.

Miss Dennis. That's funny, isn't it?

Victoria. I flatter myself there are not many women who've been married to two D.S.O.s. I think I've done my bit.

Miss Dennis. I should just think you had. If it's not asking too much, I should like to know which of them you liked best.

Victoria. Well, you know, I really can't say.

Miss Dennis. Of course, I haven't had the experience, but I should have thought you'd prefer the one who wasn't there. That almost seems like human nature, doesn't it?

Victoria. The fact is, all men have their faults. They're selfish, brutal, and inconsiderate. They don't understand how much everything costs. They can't *see* things, poor dears; they're cat-witted. Of course, Freddie's very unreasonable sometimes, but then so was Bill. And he adores me. He can hardly bear me out of his sight. They both adored me.

Miss Dennis. That makes up for a great deal, I must say.

Victoria. I can't understand the women who complain that they're misunderstood. I don't want to be understood. I want to be loved.

(Taylor, *the maid, enters up* c.)

TAYLOR (*announcing*). Mrs Shuttleworth.

(MRS SHUTTLEWORTH *enters up* C. *She is* VICTORIA's *mother and is elderly and grey haired. She is dressed in black outdoor clothes, and carries a muff.* TAYLOR *exits up* C.)

VICTORIA (*gushingly*). Darling Mother.

MRS SHUTTLEWORTH (*moving above the sofa*). My precious child. (*She leans over the back of the sofa and kisses* VICTORIA.)

VICTORIA. This is Miss Dennis. It's the only moment in the day she was able to give me.

MRS SHUTTLEWORTH (*graciously*). How do you do. (*She moves to* R. *of the table, puts her muff on the armchair and takes off her gloves.*)

MISS DENNIS. How do you do.

VICTORIA. You don't mind coming up all these stairs, do you, darling? You see, we have to be dreadfully economical with our coal. We tried to wangle more, but we couldn't manage it.

MRS SHUTTLEWORTH. Oh, I know. The coal controller was positively rude to me. Red tape, you know.

VICTORIA. They say we can only have two fires. Of course, we have to have one in the nursery, and I must have one in my bedroom. So I have to see people in here.

MRS SHUTTLEWORTH. And how are the precious darlings? (*She picks up her muff, moves to* L. *of the bed and puts her gloves and muff on it.*)

VICTORIA. Fred's got a slight cold, and Nannie thought he'd better stay in bed, but Baby's splendid. Nannie will bring him in presently.

MISS DENNIS. Are they both boys, Mrs Lowndes?

VICTORIA. Yes. But I'm going to have a girl next time.

MRS SHUTTLEWORTH. Fred will be two next month, Victoria.

VICTORIA. I know. I'm beginning to feel so old. Poor lamb, he wasn't born till three months after his father was killed.

MISS DENNIS. How very sad. You don't like the nails too red, do you?

VICTORIA. Not too red.

MRS SHUTTLEWORTH. She looked too sweet in mourning. (*She moves to the dressing-table.*) I wish you could have seen her, Miss Dennis. (*She picks up the hand-mirror and tidies her hair.*)

VICTORIA. Mother, how can you say anything so heartless? Of course, black does suit me. There's no denying that.

MRS SHUTTLEWORTH. I insisted on her going to *Mathilde*. Mourning *must* be well made, or else it looks nothing at all.

MISS DENNIS (*to* VICTORIA). Did you say your little boy's name was Fred? After his father, I suppose?

VICTORIA. Oh no, my first husband was called William. He particularly wanted the baby to be called Frederick after Major Lowndes. You see, Major Lowndes had been my husband's best man, and they'd always been such great friends.

MISS DENNIS. Oh, I see.

VICTORIA. Then, when I married Major Lowndes, and my second baby was born, we thought it would be nice to give it my first husband's name, and so we called it William.

MRS SHUTTLEWORTH (*replacing the mirror on the dressing-table*). I was against it myself. I thought it would always remind the dear child of what she'd lost.

VICTORIA. Oh, but, Mother darling, I don't feel a bit like that about Bill. I shall never forget him. (*To* MISS DENNIS.) You see, (*she points to the double photograph on the console table up* C.) I have their photographs side by side.

MISS DENNIS. Some men wouldn't like that very much.

VICTORIA. Freddie has me now. He can't grudge it if I give a passing thought to that poor dead hero who's lying in a nameless grave in France.

MRS SHUTTLEWORTH (*moving to the armchair* C.). Don't upset yourself, darling. (*She sits.*) You know how bad it is for your skin. (*To* MISS DENNIS.) She has such a soft heart, poor dear.

VICTORIA. Of course, now the war's over, it's different, but when Freddie was at the front I always thought it must be a consolation to him to think that if anything happened to him and I married again I should always keep a little corner in my heart for him.

MISS DENNIS (*rising*). There, I think that's all for today, Mrs Lowndes. Would you like me to come again on Friday? (*She collects her materials together from the stool, moves the stool down* L., *then moves above the table and packs up her case.*)

VICTORIA (*looking at her nails*). Please. (*She rises.*) You do them beautifully. There's something very satisfactory in a well-manicured hand. It gives you a sense of assurance, doesn't it? (*She moves to the fireplace.*) If I were a man I would never want to hold a hand that wasn't nicely manicured.

MISS DENNIS. The gentleman I'm going to marry said to me that the first thing that attracted him was the way my nails was polished.

VICTORIA. One never knows what'll take a man's fancy.

MRS SHUTTLEWORTH. Personally, I am a firm believer in first impressions. And that is why I say to all the girls I know, "Whenever you are being shown into a drawing-room bite both your lips hard, give them a good lick, put your head in the air, and then sail in." There's nothing men like more than a red moist mouth. I'm an old woman now, but I never go into a room without doing it.

MISS DENNIS. Fancy now, I never thought of that. I must try it and see.

MRS SHUTTLEWORTH. It may make all the difference to your life.

VICTORIA. Miss Dennis is engaged to be married, Mother,

Mrs Shuttleworth (*to* Miss Dennis). Ah, my dear, don't make the common mistake of thinking that because you've got one man safe you need not make yourself attractive to others.

Victoria. On Friday next, then, Miss Dennis.

Miss Dennis. Very well, Mrs Lowndes. (*She moves to the stool at the foot of the bed and picks up her handbag.*) Is there anything you're wanting just at the moment? (*She moves above the table.*)

Victoria. Nothing, thanks.

Miss Dennis. I've got a new skin food that they've just sent me over from Paris. I would like you to give it a trial. I think it's just the thing for your complexion.

Victoria. I'm afraid to try anything I don't know. (*She looks at herself in the mirror over the mantelpiece.*) I've got such a delicate skin.

Miss Dennis. It's been specially prepared for skins like yours, Mrs Lowndes. The ordinary skin food is well enough for the ordinary skin, but a really beautiful skin like yours wants something very extra-special in the way of food.

Victoria (*turning*). I expect it's frightfully expensive, and you know, they say we must economize. I suppose somebody's got to pay for the war.

Miss Dennis. I'll make special terms for you, Mrs Lowndes. I'll only charge you fifty-nine and six for a three-guinea pot. It's a large pot, as large as that. (*She measures with her fingers a pot about three inches high.*) I promise you it's not an extravagance. A good skin food is an investment.

Victoria. Oh, well, bring it with you next time you come.

Miss Dennis (*picking up her case*). I'm sure you won't regret it. (*She moves to the door* c.) Good afternoon, Mrs Lowndes. (*To* Mrs Shuttleworth.) Good afternoon.

(*She exits up* c.)

Mrs Shuttleworth. I dare say she's right. They pick up a lot of experience, those women. I always say the same thing to girls, "Look after your skin, and your bills will look after themselves."

Victoria (*crossing to the dressing-table*). She was telling me that the Johnston-Blakes are going to divorce.

Mrs Shuttleworth (*without concern*). Really. (*She rises.*) Why? (*She moves to the fireplace and stands with her back to it.*)

Victoria (*sitting at the dressing-table*). He's been fighting for the last four years. He says he wants a little peace now. (*She combs and tidies her hair.*)

Mrs Shuttleworth. I'm afraid many of these men who've been away so long will have got out of the habit of being married. I dare say it was a mercy that poor Bill was killed.

Victoria (*turning in her chair and facing* Mrs Shuttleworth). Mother darling, how can you say anything so dreadful?

MRS SHUTTLEWORTH. Well, I must say I was thankful when Freddie got a job at the War Office. The difference between men and women is that men are not naturally addicted to matrimony. With patience, firmness, and occasional rewards you can train them to it just as you can train a dog to walk on its hind legs. But a dog would rather walk on all fours and a man would rather be free. Marriage is a habit.

VICTORIA (*turning to face the mirror*). And a very good one, Mother.

MRS SHUTTLEWORTH. Of course. But the unfortunate thing about this world is that good habits are so much easier to get out of than bad ones.

VICTORIA. Well, one thing I do know, and that is that Freddie simply adores being married to me.

MRS SHUTTLEWORTH. In your place, I should have married Leicester Paton.

VICTORIA (*rising*). Good heavens, why? (*She moves to the sofa and sits on it.*)

MRS SHUTTLEWORTH. Have you never noticed that he wears spats? Men who wear spats always make the best husbands.

VICTORIA. It probably only means that he has cold feet. I expect he wears bedsocks, and I should hate that.

MRS SHUTTLEWORTH. Nonsense. It means that he has a neat and orderly mind. He likes things just so. Everything in its place and at the proper season. In fact, a creature of habit. I am convinced that after six months of marriage Leicester Paton would forget that he'd ever been a bachelor.

VICTORIA. I was a soldier's widow. I don't think it would have been very patriotic to marry a civilian.

MRS SHUTTLEWORTH. You girls all talked as though the war would last for ever. Heroism is all very well, but at a party it's not nearly so useful as a faculty for small talk.

(TAYLOR *enters up* C.)

TAYLOR. Mr Leicester Paton has called, madam. I said I didn't know if you could see him.

VICTORIA. Talk of the devil. Oh yes, bring him up here.

TAYLOR. Very good, madam.

(*She exits up* C.)

MRS SHUTTLEWORTH. I didn't know you were seeing anything of him, Victoria.

VICTORIA (*with some archness*). He's been rather attentive lately.

MRS SHUTTLEWORTH (*crossing to* R.). I knew I was right. (*She takes off her hat and puts it on the bed.*) I felt sure you attracted him.

VICTORIA. Oh, darling, you know I can never think of anyone but Freddie, but of course it's useful to have someone to run errands for one. And he can wangle almost anything one wants.

Mrs Shuttleworth. Butter?

Victoria. Everything, my dear, butter, sugar, whisky.

Mrs Shuttleworth. Bite your lips, darling, and give them a good lick.

(Victoria *carries out the suggestion*.)

You missed the chance of your life.

Victoria. After all, he never asked me.

Mrs Shuttleworth. Don't be silly, Victoria, you should have made him.

Victoria. You know that I adored Freddie. Besides, ration books hadn't come in then.

Mrs Shuttleworth (*moving to the chair at the dressing-table*). By the way, where is Freddie? (*She turns the chair to face* c. *and sits*.)

Victoria (*putting up her feet on the sofa*). Oh, my dear, I'm perfectly furious with him. He promised to take me out to luncheon, and he never turned up. He never telephoned or anything; not a word. I think it's too bad of him. He may be dead for all I know.

Mrs Shuttleworth. Optimist.

(Taylor *enters up* c.)

Taylor (*announcing*). Mr Leicester Paton.

(Leicester Paton *enters up* c. *He is a small, fat man, very well pleased with the world and with himself. He is beautifully dressed and is obviously prosperous. You could tell at a mile that he had so much money that he did not know what to do with it. He is affable, gallant and easy.* Taylor *exits up* c.)

Victoria. I hope you don't mind being dragged up all these stairs. (*She puts out her right hand over the back of the sofa to* Paton.)

(Paton *moves to* R. *of the sofa and kisses* Victoria's *hand*.)

We have to be so dreadfully economical with our coal. I can only afford to have a fire in my bedroom.

Paton. You're not going to tell me that you have any trouble about getting coal. (*He moves to* Mrs Shuttleworth.) Why on earth didn't you let me know? (*He shakes hands with* Mrs Shuttleworth.) How do you do?

Victoria. You don't mean to say you could get me some?

Paton (*moving above the armchair*). It's quite out of the question that a pretty woman shouldn't have everything she wants.

Victoria. I told Freddie that I felt sure he could wangle it somehow. What's the use of being at the War Office if you can't have some sort of a pull?

Paton (*taking a pencil from his pocket*). Leave it to me. (*He makes a note on his cuff*.) I'll see what I can do for you.

Victoria. You're a perfect marvel.

PATON. Now that these men are coming back from the front no-one would look at us poor devils who stayed at home if we didn't at least make ourselves useful.

VICTORIA. You only stayed at home because it was your duty.

PATON. I attested, you know; I didn't wait to be called up. But the Government said to me, "You're a ship-builder: go on building ships." So I built them ships.

MRS SHUTTLEWORTH. I think it was very noble of you.

PATON. And then they bring in a tax on excess profits. As I said to the Prime Minister myself, "It's trying one's patriotism rather high. It really is."

MRS SHUTTLEWORTH. A little bird has whispered to me that the Government intends to show its appreciation of your great services in the next Honours List.

PATON (drawing the armchair a little up C.). Oh, one doesn't ask for that. (He sits in the armchair.) One's glad to have been able to do one's bit.

VICTORIA. How true that is. That's just what I feel.

MRS SHUTTLEWORTH. Victoria has worked like a dog, you know. It's a marvel to me how her health has stood it.

VICTORIA. I don't know how many committees I've been on. I've sold at twenty-three bazaars.

PATON. There's nothing that takes it out of one so much.

VICTORIA. At the beginning of the war I worked in a canteen, but I had to give that up, because I could never go out to lunch anywhere. I thought at one time of working in a hospital, but you know all the red tape there is in those places—they said I had no training.

MRS SHUTTLEWORTH. I'm sure you'd have made a wonderful nurse.

VICTORIA. I didn't propose to be the ordinary sort of nurse at all. I was quite content to leave that to those unfortunate females who make their living by it. But it doesn't want any particular training to be nice to those poor, dear, wounded boys, to shake out their pillows, and take them flowers, and read to them. It only wants sympathy.

PATON. I don't know anyone who has more.

VICTORIA (with a flash of her eyes). With people I like.

MRS SHUTTLEWORTH. Have you stopped your teas, darling?

VICTORIA. Oh yes, after the Armistice.

PATON. You used to give teas to wounded soldiers?

VICTORIA. Yes, Tommies, you know. I think it's so important to cultivate the personal relation. I used to invite a dozen every Thursday. At first I had them in the drawing-room, but it made them shy, poor dears, so I thought it would be nicer for them if they had it in the servants' hall. I'm the only woman I know who never had the smallest trouble with her maids.

MRS SHUTTLEWORTH (rising). Darling, I think I'll go upstairs and see how my dear little grandson is. I do hope it's not influenza.

(PATON *rises, moves to the door up* C. *and opens it.*)

VICTORIA. Yes, do, Mother. He'll be thrilled to see you.

(MRS SHUTTLEWORTH *exits up* C. PATON *closes the door then moves to* R. *of the sofa.*)

PATON. Is anything the matter with your little boy?
VICTORIA. Poor darling, he's got a cold.
PATON. I'm so sorry.
VICTORIA. I dare say it's nothing, but you know what a mother is: she can't help feeling anxious.
PATON. You're a wonderful mother——
VICTORIA. I adore my children.
PATON. —and a perfect wife.
VICTORIA. D'you think so?
PATON. Doesn't your husband?
VICTORIA. Oh, he's only my husband. His opinion doesn't count.
PATON. Does he know what a lucky man he is?
VICTORIA. If he does he's quite convinced that he deserves to be.
PATON. I envy him.
VICTORIA (*flashing a glance at him*). You don't think I'm quite detestable, then?
PATON. Shall I tell you what I think of you?
VICTORIA. No, don't, you'll only exaggerate. You know there are only two qualities that I flatter myself on: I'm not vain and I am unselfish.

(MAJOR FREDERICK LOWNDES, D.S.O., *enters up* C. *He is a tall, soldierly fellow in uniform, with red tabs and a number of ribbons on his tunic. He nods to* PATON *and shakes hands with him.*)

Freddie, where *have* you been all this time?
FREDERICK. I've been at the club.
VICTORIA. But you promised to take me out to luncheon.
FREDERICK. Did I? I forgot all about it. I'm so sorry. (*He moves to the dressing-table and takes a cigarette from the box on it.*)
VICTORIA. Forgot? I suppose something more amusing turned up.
FREDERICK. Well, I only said I'd come if I wasn't too busy.
VICTORIA. Were you busy?
FREDERICK. I was.
VICTORIA. Bill was never too busy to give me luncheon when I wanted it.
FREDERICK. Fancy that.

PATON. I think I'll be getting along. Now the war's over you fellows can take things easily. My work goes on just the same.

FREDERICK. That's a new car you've got, isn't it?

PATON. I have to get about somehow, you know.

FREDERICK. So do I, but being only a soldier I manage to do it on my flat feet.

PATON (*shaking hands with* VICTORIA). Good-bye.

VICTORIA. Good-bye. So nice of you to come and see me.

(PATON *exits up* C.)

I should be glad to know why you threw me over like that.

FREDERICK (*crossing below the sofa to the fireplace*). Are you obliged to receive visitors in your bedroom? (*He takes the box of matches off the mantelpiece and lights his cigarette.*)

VICTORIA. You don't mean to say you're jealous, darling? I thought you seemed grumpy. Is he put out? Let him come and give his little wife a nice kiss.

FREDERICK (*irritably*). I'm not in the least jealous.

VICTORIA. You silly old thing. You know it's the only room in the house that's got a fire.

FREDERICK (*crossing to the stool at the foot of the bed*). Why the dickens don't you have one in the drawing-room?

VICTORIA. My poor lamb, have you forgotten that there's been a war and there happens to be a shortage of coal? I will tell you exactly why we don't have a fire in the drawing-room. Patriotism.

FREDERICK (*sitting on the stool*). Patriotism be hanged. The place is like an ice-house.

VICTORIA. Darling, don't be unreasonable. After spending two winters in the trenches I shouldn't have thought you'd be such a slave to your comfort. I know you don't mean it when you say patriotism be hanged, but you shouldn't say things like that even in jest.

FREDERICK. I'm dashed if I can see why it would be less patriotic to have a fire in the drawing-room where we could all benefit by it, rather than here where it's no good to anyone but you.

VICTORIA (*opening her eyes very wide*). Darling (*she rises*), you're not going to ask me to do without a fire in my bedroom? (*She moves to the fireplace.*) How can you be so selfish? Heaven knows, I don't want to boast about anything I've done, but after having slaved my life out for four years I do think I deserve a little consideration.

FREDERICK (*rising and moving up* C.). I'll go and see the kid.

VICTORIA. And it's not as if I grudged you the use of my room. You can come and sit here as much as you like. Besides, a man has his club. He can always go there if he wants to.

FREDERICK (*turning and moving down* C.). I apologize. You're quite right. You're always right.

VICTORIA. I thought you wanted me to be happy.

FREDERICK. I do, darling.

VICTORIA. Before we were married, you said you'd make that the chief aim of your life.

FREDERICK (*smiling*). I can't imagine that a sensible man could want a better one.

VICTORIA (*beckoning to him*). Confess that you've been a perfect pig.

FREDERICK (*moving to her*). A brute beast, darling.

VICTORIA (*mollified*). D'you know that I asked you to give me a kiss just now? It's not a request that I'm in the habit of having ignored.

FREDERICK. I trust it's not one that you're in the habit of making to all and sundry. (*He kisses her.*)

VICTORIA. Now tell me why you forgot to take me out to luncheon today.

FREDERICK. I didn't forget. I was prevented. I—I haven't had any luncheon myself. I'll just (*he moves up* C.) ring and ask the cook to send me up something.

VICTORIA. My poor lamb, the cook left this morning.

FREDERICK (*stopping and turning*). Again?

VICTORIA. How d'you mean again? This is the first time she's left.

FREDERICK. Hang it all, she's only been here a week.

VICTORIA. You needn't get cross about it. It's much more annoying for me than for you.

FREDERICK (*irritably*). I don't know why on earth you can't keep your servants.

VICTORIA. No-one can keep servants nowadays.

FREDERICK. Other people do.

VICTORIA. Please don't speak to me like that, Freddie. (*She crosses to* R.) I'm not used to it.

FREDERICK (*moving down* C.). I shall speak to you exactly as I choose.

VICTORIA (*turning to him*). It's so petty to lose your temper just because you can't have something to eat. I should have thought after spending two years in the trenches you'd be accustomed to going without a meal now and then.

FREDERICK. For goodness' sake don't make a scene.

VICTORIA. It's not I who am making a scene. It's you who are making a scene.

FREDERICK. Victoria, I beg you to control yourself.

VICTORIA. I don't know how you can be so unkind to me. After all the anxiety I suffered on your account when you were in France I do think you might have a little consideration for me.

FREDERICK. Seeing that for the last year I've had a perfectly safe, cushy job at the War Office, I think you might by now have recovered from any anxiety you felt on my account.

VICTORIA. Must I remind you that my nerves were shattered by poor Bill's death?

FREDERICK. No, but I was confident you would.

VICTORIA. The doctor said I should need the greatest attention for several years. I don't believe I shall ever quite get over it. I should have thought even if you didn't love me any more you'd have a little human pity for me. That's all I ask, just the tolerant kindness you'd show to a dog who was fond of you. (*She moves above* FREDERICK, *then above the sofa and works herself into a passion.*) Heaven knows, I'm not exacting. I do everything I can to make you happy. I'm patience itself. Even my worst enemy would have to admit that I'm unselfish. (*She moves above him to* L. *of the bed.*)

FREDERICK (*over his left shoulder*). I . . . (*He turns and looks up* R. *but misses seeing her.*)

VICTORIA (*moving quickly above him to* R. *of the sofa; ignoring the interruption*). You weren't obliged to marry me. I didn't ask you to. You pretended you loved me. I would never have married you if it hadn't been for Bill. You were his greatest friend. You made me love you because you spoke so beautifully of him. (*She moves above him to* L. *of the bed.*)

FREDERICK (*turning and looking up* L.). But . . . (*He turns and looks up* R. *but misses seeing her again.*)

VICTORIA (*moving quickly above him to* R. *of the sofa; ignoring the interruption and going implacably on*). That's my mistake. I've loved you too much. You're not big enough to bear so great a love. Oh, what a fool I've been. I let myself be taken in by you and I've been bitterly punished. (*She moves below the sofa.*)

FREDERICK. Why . . .

VICTORIA (*heading off the words she sees he wants to speak*). Bill would never have treated me like that. (*She moves to* L. *of him.*) Bill wouldn't have taken my poor, loving heart and thrown it aside like an old hat. Bill loved me. He would have always loved me. I adored that man. He waited on me hand and foot. He was the most unselfish man I ever really cared for. I was mad ever to think of marrying you, mad, mad, mad. (*She crosses to* R.) I shall never be happy again. I would give anything in the world to have my dear, dear Bill back again.

FREDERICK (*moving to the fireplace*). I'm so glad you feel like that about it, because he'll be here in about three minutes.

VICTORIA (*turning to face him; startled*). What? What on earth d'you mean by that?

FREDERICK. He rang me up at the club a little while ago.

VICTORIA. Freddie! What are you talking about? Are you mad?

FREDERICK. No. Nor drunk.

VICTORIA. I don't understand. Who talked to you?

FREDERICK. Bill.

VICTORIA. Bill. Bill who?

FREDERICK. Bill Cardew.

VICTORIA. But, poor darling, he's dead.

FREDERICK (*moving to the sofa and sitting*). He showed no sign of it on the telephone.

VICTORIA. But, Freddie—Freddie. (*She moves to* R. *of the sofa.*) Oh, you're pulling my leg. It's too beastly of you. How can you be so heartless?

FREDERICK. Well, just wait and you'll see for yourself. (*He looks at his wrist-watch.*) In about two and a half minutes now, I should think.

VICTORIA (*coaxing him*). Now, Freddie, don't be vindictive. I dare say I was rather catty. I didn't mean it. You know I adore you. (*She sits in the armchair* C.) You can have a fire in your study and damn the fuel controller. I'm sorry for all I said just now. There, now, it's all right, isn't it?

FREDERICK. Perfectly. But it's not going to prevent Bill from walking into this room in about two minutes and a quarter.

VICTORIA (*rising and moving* R.). I shall scream. It's not true. Oh, Freddie, if you ever loved me, say it's not true.

FREDERICK. There's no need to take my word for it.

VICTORIA. But, Freddie darling, do be sensible. Poor Bill was killed at the Battle of Ypres. He was actually seen to fall. (*She moves to the stool at the foot of the bed.*) He was reported dead by the War Office. You know how distressed I was. I wore mourning and everything. (*She sits on the stool.*) We even had a memorial service.

FREDERICK. I know. It'll want a devil of a lot of explaining, turning up like this.

VICTORIA. I shall go stark, staring mad in a minute. How do you know it was Bill who spoke to you on the telephone?

FREDERICK. He said so.

VICTORIA (*rising*). That proves nothing. (*She moves down* R.) Lots of people say they're the Kaiser.

FREDERICK. Yes, but they speak from a lunatic asylum. He spoke from Harwich Station.

VICTORIA. I dare say it was somebody else of the same name.

FREDERICK. That's idiotic, Victoria. I recognized his voice.

VICTORIA. What did he say exactly?

FREDERICK. Well, he said he was at Harwich Station, and would be in London at three-thirteen. And would I break it to you?

VICTORIA. But he must have said more than that.

FREDERICK. No, not much.

VICTORIA (*sitting on the dressing-table chair*). For goodness' sake, tell me exactly what he said—exactly.

FREDERICK (*rising and moving to the fireplace*). Well, I was just coming along to take you out to luncheon, when I was told I was wanted on the telephone. A long-distance call—Harwich.

B

VICTORIA. I know. A seaport town.

FREDERICK. I strolled along and took up the receiver. I said, "Is that you, darling?"

VICTORIA. Why did you say that?

FREDERICK. That's always a good opening on the telephone. It puts the person at the other end at their ease.

VICTORIA. Idiot!

FREDERICK. Somebody said, "Is that you, Freddie?" I thought I recognized the voice, and I felt all funny. "Yes," I said. "It's me, Bill," he said, "Bill Cardew."

VICTORIA. For heaven's sake be quick about it.

FREDERICK. "Hulloa," I said, "I thought you were dead." "I thought as much," he answered. "How are you?" I said. "A-one," he said.

VICTORIA. What an idiotic conversation.

FREDERICK. Damn it all, I had to say something.

VICTORIA. You ought to have said a thousand things.

FREDERICK. We only had three minutes.

VICTORIA. Well, go on.

FREDERICK. He said, "I'm just tootling up to London. I'll be up at three-thirteen. You might go along and break it to Victoria." "Right-ho," I said. He said, "So long," and I said, "So long." And we rang off.

VICTORIA. But that was before luncheon. Why didn't you come at once and tell me?

FREDERICK. To tell you the truth I was a bit shaken by then. I thought the first thing was to have a double whisky and a small soda.

VICTORIA. And what did you do then?

FREDERICK (moving to the sofa). Well, I sat down to think. (He sits on the sofa.) I thought steadily for a couple of hours.

VICTORIA. And what have you thought?

FREDERICK. Nothing.

VICTORIA. It seems hardly worth while to have gone without your lunch.

FREDERICK. It's a devilish awkward position for me.

VICTORIA. For you? (She turns to face the mirror.) And what about me?

FREDERICK. After all, Bill was my oldest pal. He may think it rather funny that I've married his wife.

VICTORIA. Funny!

FREDERICK. On the other hand, he may not.

VICTORIA (shaking her finger at him in the mirror). Why didn't you tell me the moment you came in, instead of talking about heaven knows what?

FREDERICK. It wasn't a very easy thing to say. I was trying to find an opportunity to slip it in casually, don't you know.

VICTORIA (turning; furiously). Wasting precious time.

FREDERICK (*blandly*). Darling, you surely don't think making a scene is ever waste of time.

VICTORIA. Now we haven't got a chance to decide on anything. I haven't even time to put a frock on.

FREDERICK. What the deuce do you want to put a frock on for?

VICTORIA (*rising*). After all, I am his widow. (*She moves* C.) I think it would be only nice of me to be wearing mourning when he comes. What did he say when you told him?

FREDERICK (*rising and moving to the fireplace*). When I told him what?

VICTORIA. How can you be so stupid! When you told him you and I were married.

FREDERICK. But I didn't tell him.

VICTORIA. Do you mean to say that he's coming here under the impression that I'm his wife?

FREDERICK. Why, naturally.

VICTORIA. But why on earth didn't you tell him at once? It was the only thing to do. Surely you see that.

FREDERICK. It didn't strike me at the moment. Besides, it's rather a delicate thing to say on the telephone.

VICTORIA (*breaking* R.). Well, someone must tell him.

FREDERICK. I've come to the conclusion that you're quite the best person to do that.

VICTORIA (*turning*). I? Do you think I'm going to do all your dirty work?

FREDERICK. I must say, I don't think it would come well from me.

VICTORIA. I'm not going to deal my darling Bill this bitter, bitter blow.

FREDERICK (*moving above the sofa*). By the way, it's—it's jolly he's alive, isn't it?

VICTORIA (*sitting on the stool at the foot of the bed*). Ripping.

FREDERICK. I am glad, aren't you?

VICTORIA. Yes, awfully glad.

FREDERICK (*moving to* L. *of her*). Then you'll just break the news as gently as you can, Victoria.

VICTORIA (*as if she were weighing the matter*). I really don't think that's my province.

FREDERICK (*exercising all his charm*). Darling, you've got so much tact. I never knew anyone who could deal with a delicate situation as you can. You have such a light hand. You're so sympathetic. And you've got such a wonderful tenderness.

VICTORIA. I don't think you've got hold of the right line at all. There's only one way to manage a thing like this. (*She rises.*) You just take him by the arm and say, "Look here, old man, the fact is . . ."

FREDERICK (*interrupting*). Victoria, you don't mean to say

you're willing to give up the chance of making the biggest scene you've ever made in your life?

VICTORIA. Now look here, Freddie, this is the only thing I've ever asked you to do for me in my life. You know how frail I am. I'm not feeling at all well. (*She moves to the dressing-table.*) You're the only man I have to lean on.

FREDERICK. It's no good, Victoria. I won't.

VICTORIA (*furiously*). Damn you.

(*A door bell is heard to ring off.*)

FREDERICK. By George, here he is. (*He moves below the sofa.*)

VICTORIA. I've not even powdered my nose. Fortunately I have no personal vanity. (*She begins feverishly to powder herself.*)

WILLIAM (*off up* C.; *calling*). Hulloa! Hulloa! Hulloa!

(*The door up* C. *is flung open and* MAJOR WILLIAM CARDEW, D.S.O., *bursts in. He is a well-set-up, jovial fellow. He wears a very shabby civilian suit.*)

(*He moves to* VICTORIA.) Here we are again.

VICTORIA (*turning*). Bill!

FREDERICK. Was I right?

VICTORIA. I can hardly believe my eyes.

WILLIAM. Give me a kiss, old lady. (*He seizes* VICTORIA *in his arms and gives her a hearty kiss, then releases her and turns to* FREDERICK.) Well, Freddie, old man, (*he moves to* FREDERICK *and shakes hands with him*) how's life?

FREDERICK. A-one, thanks.

WILLIAM. Are you surprised to see me?

FREDERICK. A little.

VICTORIA. In fact, a good deal.

WILLIAM. I'm jolly glad to see you here, Freddie, old man. On the way up in the train I cursed myself five times for not having asked you to wait with Victoria till I rolled up. I was afraid you might have some damned feeling of delicacy.

FREDERICK. I?

WILLIAM (*moving to* L. *of* VICTORIA). You see, it struck me you might think Victoria and I would want to be alone just the first moment, but I should have been as sick as a dog if I hadn't seen your ugly old face here to welcome me. (*He moves to* R. *of* FREDER-ICK.) By the way, you've neither of you said you were glad to see me.

VICTORIA. Of course we're glad, Bill darling.

FREDERICK. Rather.

WILLIAM (*moving to* L. *of* VICTORIA). Tactful of me to get old Freddie to come round and break the news to you, I think, Victoria.

VICTORIA. Yes, darling, and exactly like you

WILLIAM. It's just like old times to hear you call me "darling" every other minute.

FREDERICK. It's one of Victoria's favourite words.

WILLIAM (*moving to* R. *of* FREDERICK). You know, I nearly didn't warn you. I thought it would be rather a lark to break in on you in the middle of the night.

(FREDERICK *and* VICTORIA *give a little start and look at each other.*)

VICTORIA. I'm just as glad you didn't do that, Bill.

(FREDERICK *breaks to the fireplace.*)

WILLIAM. What a scene, my word. The sleeping beauty on her virtuous couch. Enter a man in a shocking old suit. Shrieks of the sleeping beauty. It is I, your husband. Tableau.

VICTORIA (*to turn the conversation*). You're quite right, it is a shocking old suit. Where did you get it?

WILLIAM. I didn't get it. I pinched it. I must say I wouldn't mind getting into some decent things. (*He moves towards the door up* C.)

VICTORIA (*hastily*). Where are you going?

WILLIAM (*stopping and turning*). I was going into my dressing-room. Upon my soul, I almost forget what I've got. I had a blue serge suit that was rather dressy.

VICTORIA. I've put all your clothes away, darling.

WILLIAM (*easing above the bed and speaking across it*). Where?

VICTORIA. In camphor. You couldn't put them on until they've been aired.

WILLIAM. "Hell", said the duchess.

(MRS SHUTTLEWORTH *enters up* C. WILLIAM *is standing so that at first she does not see him.*)

MRS SHUTTLEWORTH (*moving down* R.C.). I think the little lamb is going on nicely, Victoria.

VICTORIA (*swallowing*). Mother . . .

WILLIAM. I was just going to ask about the kid.

(MRS SHUTTLEWORTH *startled, turns and sees* WILLIAM.)

MRS SHUTTLEWORTH. Who is that?

WILLIAM. Who the devil d'you think it is?

MRS SHUTTLEWORTH. The language and the voice—Bill Cardew's. Who is that?

WILLIAM (*moving down* C. *to* L. *of* MRS SHUTTLEWORTH). Well, I may be a bit thinner and it certainly is a shocking old suit.

MRS SHUTTLEWORTH. Don't come near me or I shall scream.

WILLIAM. You can't escape me. I'm going to kiss you.

MRS SHUTTLEWORTH. Take him away. (*She breaks to* L. *of* VICTORIA.) Don't let him come near me. Victoria, who is that man?

FREDERICK. Well, Mrs Shuttleworth, it's Bill Cardew.

(VICTORIA *sits on the dressing-table chair.*)

MRS SHUTTLEWORTH. But he's dead.

FREDERICK. He doesn't seem to know it.

MRS SHUTTLEWORTH. It's absurd. Will someone wake me up.

WILLIAM. Shall I pinch her, and if so, where?

MRS SHUTTLEWORTH. It's a horrible dream. Of course he's dead. That man's an imposter.

WILLIAM. Shall I show you the strawberry mark on my left shoulder?

MRS SHUTTLEWORTH. I tell you Bill Cardew's dead.

WILLIAM. Prove it.

MRS SHUTTLEWORTH (*indignantly*). Prove it? The War Office announced it officially; Victoria went into mourning.

WILLIAM. Did she look nice in it?

MRS SHUTTLEWORTH. Sweet. Perfectly sweet. Why, we had a memorial service. (*She sits on the stool at the foot of the bed.*)

FREDERICK. Fully choral.

WILLIAM. Did you have a memorial service for me, Victoria? That was nice of you.

VICTORIA. It was very well attended.

WILLIAM. I'm glad it wasn't a frost.

FREDERICK. I say, old man, we don't want to hurry you, you know, but we're all waiting for some sort of explanation.

WILLIAM. I was coming to that. I was just giving you time to get over your first raptures at seeing me again. Have you got over them?

FREDERICK. I can only speak for myself.

WILLIAM. Well, you know, I was damned badly wounded.

FREDERICK. Yes, at Ypres. A fellow saw you fall. He said you were shot through the head. He just stopped a minute, and saw you were killed, and went on.

WILLIAM. I wasn't. I was eventually picked up and taken to Germany.

VICTORIA. Why didn't you write?

WILLIAM. Well, I think I must have been rather dotty for a bit. I don't know exactly how long I was in hospital, but when I began to sit up and take nourishment I couldn't remember a damned thing. My memory had completely gone.

MRS SHUTTLEWORTH. Strange. To my mind very strange!

WILLIAM (*moving to* L. *of* MRS SHUTTLEWORTH). I think my wound must have made me a bit irritable. When I was being taken along to a camp I had a difference of opinion with a German officer, and I laid him out. (*He moves down* L.C.) By George, they sentenced me to about a hundred and fifty years' imprisonment, and prevented me from writing, or making any sign that I was alive.

VICTORIA. But your memory came back?

WILLIAM. Yes, gradually. And, of course, I realized then that you'd think I was dead. But I had no means of letting you know.

FREDERICK. You might have wired from Rotterdam.

WILLIAM (*sitting in the armchair* C.). The lines were so congested. They told me I'd arrive before my wire.

MRS SHUTTLEWORTH. It's all quite probable.

WILLIAM. More or less, I flatter myself. But you can bet your life on one thing; I'm not dead, and what's more, I propose to live for another forty years, if not fifty.

(TAYLOR *enters up* C.)

TAYLOR. If you please, ma'am, where shall I put the gentleman's things? He told me to bring them upstairs.

WILLIAM (*rising and turning*). Oh, it's only a few odds and ends for the journey that I got on my way. (*He moves up* C.) Put them in the dressing-room.

VICTORIA. No, leave that for the moment, Taylor. We'll decide presently.

TAYLOR. Very good, madam.

(*She exits up* C.)

WILLIAM. What's the matter with the dressing-room, Victoria?

VICTORIA. My poor darling, don't forget your arrival is a complete surprise. Nothing is ready.

WILLIAM. Don't let that worry you. (*He moves above the bed.*) After what I've been used to, I can pig it anywhere. (*He looks at the bed.*) By George, a spring mattress. Father will sleep without rocking tonight.

MRS SHUTTLEWORTH (*rising and crossing to* FREDERICK; *firmly*). Something's got to be done.

WILLIAM. How d'you mean?

VICTORIA (*hurriedly*). We haven't got a cook.

WILLIAM. Oh, you needn't bother about that. Freddie and I will do the cooking. My speciality is a grilled steak. What can you do, Freddie?

FREDERICK. I can boil an egg.

WILLIAM. Splendid. They always say that's the one thing a chef can't do. Nothing to worry about. (*He moves down* R.C.) We'll get in some *pâté-de-foie-gras*, a few oysters, and there you are. Now let's have a look at the kid.

MRS SHUTTLEWORTH (*moving to the armchair*). He's not very well today. (*She sits.*) I don't think he should leave his bed.

WILLIAM. Oh, all right. I'll toddle up and see him. (*He eases* C.) I haven't made his lordship's acquaintance yet. (*He moves to* VICTORIA.) What's his name?

VICTORIA (*rather nervously*). Don't you remember, just before you went away, you said you'd like him called Frederick if he was a boy?

WILLIAM. Yes, I know I did, but you said you'd see me damned. You'd quite made up your mind to call him Lancelot.

VICTORIA. When I thought you were dead I felt I must respect your wishes.

WILLIAM. It must have been a shock if it took you like that.

VICTORIA. Of course, I asked Freddie to be godfather.

WILLIAM. Has the old ruffian been a standby to you while I've been away?

VICTORIA. I—I've seen a good deal of him.

WILLIAM. I felt you were safe with him, you know. He's a brick.

FREDERICK. I say, you might spare my blushes while you're about it.

VICTORIA. He was very kind to me during my—bereavement.

WILLIAM. Dear old chap. (*To* FREDERICK.) I knew you were a tower of strength.

FREDERICK (*sweating freely*). I—I did what I could, you know.

WILLIAM. Well, don't be so modest about it.

MRS SHUTTLEWORTH (*more firmly*). I tell you something must be done.

WILLIAM. My dear Victoria, what is the matter with your mother?

FREDERICK (*trying to change the conversation*). I think we might bust ourselves and have some bubbly tonight, Victoria.

WILLIAM. And damn the expense.

FREDERICK. I wonder if it's arrived yet. I told them to send a case in the day before yesterday.

WILLIAM. Have you been running the cellar? Rash to let him do that, Victoria, very rash.

VICTORIA. I know nothing about wine.

WILLIAM. Freddie knows a thing or two. (*He crosses to* FREDERICK.) I say, do you remember that last time we went on a bat together? You were blind to the world.

FREDERICK (*turning to the fireplace*). Go to blazes! I was nothing of the sort.

WILLIAM. Pretty little thing that was. Are you as thick with her as you used to be?

(VICTORIA *draws herself up and looks daggers at* FREDERICK.)

FREDERICK (*turning; with dignity*). I haven't an idea who you're referring to.

WILLIAM. Oh, my dear old boy, don't put any frills on. Victoria's a married woman, and she knows what the lads of the village are when they get out. (*He crosses to* VICTORIA.) A very nice little girl indeed, Victoria. If I hadn't been a married man I'd have had a shot at cutting Freddie out.

VICTORIA (*icily*). He always told me he'd never looked at a woman in his life.

WILLIAM. You shouldn't encourage the young to lie. That's what they all say. Rapid. These wretched aeroplane fellows have been turning out engine after engine, and they can't keep pace with him. Talk of a lurid past; Mrs Shuttleworth, veil your face.

FREDERICK. My poor Bill, your memory! When you recovered it, I'm afraid you remembered all sorts of things that had never happened.

WILLIAM. Past, did I say? Unless I'm very much mistaken, his present wouldn't bear the closest inspection.

FREDERICK. By George, I've hit it. The poor fellow thinks he's being funny.

WILLIAM (*going on*). I don't blame you. Make hay while the sun shines. I admire the way you can make love to three women at a time and make each one believe she's the only one you've ever really cared for.

MRS SHUTTLEWORTH (*rising; with determination*). If someone doesn't do something at once I shall do it myself.

WILLIAM (*indicating* MRS SHUTTLEWORTH; *in a significant whisper to* VICTORIA). Air raids?

(*A baby's wail is heard off.*)

VICTORIA (*agitatedly*). Willie.

WILLIAM. Hulloa, what's that? Is that the kid? (*He moves quickly to the door up* C. *and opens it.*)

(*The wailing becomes louder.*)

(*He looks off.*) Why, it's coming upstairs. You told me the kid was in the nursery. (*He calls off.*) Bring him along and let me have a look at him.

(NANNIE *enters up* C. *She wears a neat grey uniform and carries a baby in her arms. She moves to* VICTORIA.)

VICTORIA (*rising; desperately*). Freddie, do something, even if it's only something stupid.

FREDERICK. The only thing that occurs to me is to stand on my head.

(WILLIAM *moves to* L. *of* NANNIE *and peers at the baby.*)

WILLIAM (*jovially*). Hulloa, hulloa, hulloa.

FREDERICK. That's not the way to talk to a baby, you owl.

WILLIAM. Not such a baby as all that. Can he speak yet, Nannie?

NANNIE. Oh no, sir, not yet.

WILLIAM. Rather backward, isn't he? Not what I should have expected in a son of mine.

(NANNIE *gives* WILLIAM *a look of surprise, and then with a look at* VICTORIA, *assumes an appearance of extreme primness.*)

NANNIE. I never knew a baby talk as young as that, sir.

WILLIAM. Upon my soul, there's not much of him. Looks to me rather a stumer. I think we've been done, Victoria.

NANNIE (*indignantly*). Oh, I don't think you ought to say that, sir. He's a very fine boy. He weighs more than a good many do when they're six months.

WILLIAM. What's that? How old is he?

NANNIE. Four months last Tuesday, sir.

WILLIAM. You've been busy in my absence, Victoria.

VICTORIA. Freddie, for goodness' sake speak. Don't stand there like a stuffed tomato.

MRS SHUTTLEWORTH. Leave the room, Nannie.

(NANNIE, *pursing her lips, intrigued and perplexed, exits up* C., *taking the baby with her.*)

FREDERICK (*crossing to* WILLIAM; *trying to take it lightly*). The fact is, you've made rather an absurd mistake. You've been away so long that of course there's a good deal you don't know.

WILLIAM. I'm a simple creature.

FREDERICK. Well, to cut a long story short . . .

WILLIAM. What story?

FREDERICK. I wish you wouldn't interrupt me. I'm telling you as quickly as I can. To cut a long story short, the infant that's just gone out of the room is not your son.

WILLIAM. I had a sort of suspicion he wasn't. I tell you that frankly.

VICTORIA. Oh, the fool. The blithering nincompoop.

WILLIAM. Well, who the deuce is his father?

FREDERICK. In point of fact, I am.

WILLIAM. You? You don't mean to say you're married?

FREDERICK. Lots of people are. In fact, marriage has been quite the thing during the war.

WILLIAM. Why on earth didn't you tell me?

FREDERICK. Hang it all, man, you've been dead for the last three years. How could I?

WILLIAM (*seizing* FREDERICK'S *hand*). Well, I'm jolly glad to hear it, old chap. I knew you'd be caught one of these days. You were a wily old bird, but—ah, well, we all come to it. My very best congratulations.

FREDERICK. That's awfully good of you. I'm—er—I'm staying here, you know.

WILLIAM. Are you? That's first rate. Is your missus here, too?

FREDERICK. It's rather difficult to explain.

WILLIAM. Don't tell me she's only got one eye.

FREDERICK. Can't you guess why I'm staying here?

WILLIAM. No. (*He looks around the room and his eyes fall on* MRS SHUTTLEWORTH.) You don't mean to say you've married Victoria's mother?

(MRS SHUTTLEWORTH *moves to the fireplace.*)

FREDERICK. No, not exactly.

WILLIAM (*crossing to* MRS SHUTTLEWORTH). What does he mean by not exactly? I hope you haven't been trifling with the affections of my mother-in-law?

MRS SHUTTLEWORTH. Do I look as if I were the mother of that baby?

WILLIAM. We live in an age of progress. One should keep an open mind about things.

FREDERICK. You quite misunderstand me, Bill.

WILLIAM. Is there nothing between you and Victoria's mother?

FREDERICK. Certainly not.

WILLIAM. Well, I'm sorry. I should have liked to be your son-in-law. And you would have done the right thing by her, wouldn't you?

VICTORIA. Really, Bill, I don't think you should talk about my mother like that.

WILLIAM. If he's compromised her he ought to marry her.

VICTORIA. He hasn't compromised her and he can't marry her.

WILLIAM. I don't want to seem inquisitive, but if you didn't marry Victoria's mother, who did you marry?

FREDERICK. Damn you, I married Victoria.

CURTAIN.

ACT II

SCENE.—*The drawing-room. The following morning.*

The décor of the room is very bizarre. It has been carried out by an artist in futurism, and the result is very modern, outrageous and fantastic, but not ugly. The entrance is L. *of a raised alcove up* L. *approached by two steps. There is a window in the* R. *wall of the alcove. A large bay, with window* R. *and* L. *of it, stretches from* R. *of the alcove steps to the wall* R. *The bay is fronted by a draped arch supported on square pillars* R. *and* L. *of it. The fireplace is down* R. *A writing desk, backed by a decorated screen, stands down* L., *with a small chair to it. A standard lamp with an elaborate shade stands* L. *of the alcove steps. The alcove is dressed with a pedestal on which stands a large vase filled with feather palm or grasses. The bay is furnished with a red plush love seat* C. *of it, a table* L. *of it, on which stands a gramophone, and a chair* R. *of it. A small settee stands* R. *above the fireplace, with a small table* R. *of it on which there is a tall Chinese vase. There is a small chair down* R., *below the fireplace. A small circular table with an armchair* L. *of it stands* C. *The floor carpet is red with beige carpet on the alcove floor and steps. The drapes on the arch of the bay are of a heavy mauve material. The walls are decorated with unusual pictures, fans, etc. At night, the room is lit by a pendant hanging* C. *of the arch and candle-lamp wall-brackets over the mantelpiece.*

(See the Ground Plan at the end of the Play.)

When the CURTAIN *rises, the fire is set but not alight. All the windows are open.* FREDERICK *is seated on the settee. He has changed to civilian clothes. He wears an overcoat and has a rug wrapped round his knees and legs. He is reading the morning newspaper.* MRS SHUTTLEWORTH *enters up* L. *She wears her outdoor clothes and carries her gloves.*

MRS SHUTTLEWORTH (*putting her gloves on the table* C.). I'm going now.

FREDERICK. Are you?

MRS SHUTTLEWORTH. I'm taking my dear little grandchildren away with me.

FREDERICK. Are you?

MRS SHUTTLEWORTH. Victoria will be down presently.

FREDERICK. Will she?

MRS SHUTTLEWORTH. I should have thought you'd ask how she was after that dreadful shock.

FREDERICK. Would you?

MRS SHUTTLEWORTH (*crossing to the fireplace*). You don't seem in a very good temper this morning. (*She adjusts her hat in the mirror over the mantelpiece.*)

FREDERICK. I'm not.

MRS SHUTTLEWORTH. She's better, poor darling, but she's terribly shaken. I put her to bed at once with hot-water bottles.

FREDERICK. Did you?

MRS SHUTTLEWORTH. Of course, she was totally unfit to discuss this terrible situation yesterday.

FREDERICK. Was she?

MRS SHUTTLEWORTH. Surely you can see that for yourself. The only thing was to keep her perfectly quiet till she'd had time to recover a little.

FREDERICK. Was it?

MRS SHUTTLEWORTH (*crossing to the table* C.). But this morning I have no doubt you'll find her prepared to go into the matter.

FREDERICK. Shall I?

MRS SHUTTLEWORTH. If you have nothing else you wish to say to me I think I'll go now. (*She picks up her gloves.*)

FREDERICK. Will you?

(MRS SHUTTLEWORTH *purses her lips very tight.* TAYLOR *enters up* L.)

TAYLOR. Mr Leicester Paton has called, madam. Mrs Lowndes says, will you see him a minute. She's just getting out of her bath.

MRS SHUTTLEWORTH. Certainly. Show him in here.

TAYLOR. Very good, madam.

(*She exits up* L.)

FREDERICK. I'll go.

MRS SHUTTLEWORTH (*sitting in the armchair* C.). I wonder what he wants.

FREDERICK (*rising*). Perhaps he wants Victoria's permission to pay you his addresses.

(*He exits up* L., *taking the rug and newspaper with him.* TAYLOR *enters up* L.)

TAYLOR (*announcing*). Mr Leicester Paton.

(PATON *enters up* L. TAYLOR *exits up* L.)

PATON (*moving* C.). Your daughter rang me up this morning. I thought the best thing I could do was to come along at once.

MRS SHUTTLEWORTH. That's too good of you. I'm sure if anything can be done you are the man to do it.

PATON (*putting his hat and gloves on the table* C.). It's an extraordinary situation. (*He moves to the fireplace and stands with his back to it.*)

MRS SHUTTLEWORTH. Of course, I think it was very inconsiderate of Bill to turn up like that.

PATON. Poor thing, she must be quite upset.

MRS SHUTTLEWORTH. Well, I can only tell you that the shock entirely took the wave out of her hair. She only had it done yesterday, and it was as straight as a telegraph pole this morning.

PATON. You don't say so.

(VICTORIA *enters up* L. *She has on her dressing-gown and bedroom slippers. Her hair is only partly done, but she manages to look perfectly ravishing.*)

VICTORIA (*as she enters*). I didn't want to keep you waiting.

MRS SHUTTLEWORTH. Here she is.

(PATON *moves to* L. *of the settee.*)

VICTORIA (*crossing below* PATON *to the fireplace*). I came down just as I was. You mustn't look at me.

PATON. I can't help it.

VICTORIA. What nonsense. (*She sits on the settee at the* R. *end of it.*) I know I look a perfect fright, but fortunately I have no personal vanity.

PATON (*sitting* L. *of* VICTORIA *on the settee and holding her hand*). What a catastrophe! You must be beside yourself.

VICTORIA (*with a charming smile*). I knew I could rely on your sympathy.

PATON. What in heaven's name are you going to do?

VICTORIA. It's because I haven't an idea that I telephoned to you. You see, you've taught me to bring all my difficulties to you.

PATON. To whom else should you bring them? We must think. We must discuss the matter.

VICTORIA. The position is impossible.

PATON. It's wonderful that you bear it so bravely. I was expecting to find you in a state of collapse.

VICTORIA (*with a flash of the eyes*). With you to lean on?

PATON. I suppose you've been having the most terrible scenes.

VICTORIA. Heartrending. You see, they both adore me.

PATON. And you?

VICTORIA. I? I only want to do—my duty.

PATON. How like you! How exactly like you.

MRS SHUTTLEWORTH (*rising*). If there's nothing more I can do for you, darling, I think I'll go now.

(PATON *rises and moves to* L. *of the settee.*)

VICTORIA. Do, darling.

MRS SHUTTLEWORTH (*shaking hands with* PATON). Be very kind to her.

PATON. I'll try.

(MRS SHUTTLEWORTH *exits up* L.)

VICTORIA (*almost tenderly*). It was sweet of you to come and see me at once. I was afraid you wouldn't have time.

PATON. Do you imagine I should allow anything to stand in the way when you sent for me?

VICTORIA. Oh, but you know I shouldn't like to think that you were putting yourself out on my account.

PATON. I wish I could pretend I were. As a matter of fact, I was only going down to see a place I've just bought in the country, and as I wanted to try my new Rolls I thought I'd kill two birds with one stone.

VICTORIA (*easing along the seat to the* L. *end of the settee*). I didn't know you were buying a place.

PATON. Oh, it's a very modest little affair. The park is not more than three hundred acres, and there are only twenty-eight bedrooms. But you see, I'm a bachelor. I want so little.

VICTORIA. Where is it?

PATON. It's near Newmarket.

VICTORIA. A very nice neighbourhood.

PATON. A man in my position is bound to do something for the good of the country, and it seems to me that to patronize a good old English sport, which gives employment to numbers of respectable men, is an occupation which is truly patriotic. I'm going to take up racing.

VICTORIA. I think it's splendid of you. So many men waste their money on their own selfish pleasures. It's such a relief to come across anyone who is determined to make a thoroughly good use of it. I've often wondered that you didn't go into Parliament.

PATON. For the last four years I've been too busy winning the war to bother about governing the nation.

VICTORIA. Yes, but now. They want strong men of keen intelligence and dominating personality.

PATON. It's not impossible that very soon I shall have the opportunity to show of what metal I am made. But not in the House of Commons.

VICTORIA (*all to pieces*). In the House of Lords?

PATON (*roguishly*). Ah, you mustn't ask me to betray the confidence of the Prime Minister.

VICTORIA. You'll look sweet in scarlet and ermine.

PATON (*crossing to the fireplace; gallantly*). But it's too bad of me to talk about my concerns when yours are so much more important.

VICTORIA. Oh, you can't think how I love to hear you talk about yourself. One feels a brain behind every word you say.

PATON. It's easy to be brilliant when one has a sympathetic listener.

VICTORIA. Of course, Bill and Freddie are dear, good fellows, but their conversation is a little limited. During the war it was rather smart to talk about guns, and flying machines, and fleabags, but now . . .

PATON. I understand you so well, dear lady.

VICTORIA. Why do you call me that?

PATON. Out of pure embarrassment. I don't know whether to call you Mrs Cardew or Mrs Lowndes.

VICTORIA. Why don't you split the difference and call me Victoria?

PATON (*sitting* R. *of* VICTORIA *on the settee*). May I?

VICTORIA (*giving him her left hand*). It will make me feel that you are not an entire stranger to me.

PATON (*with surprise*). Your wedding rings? You always used to wear two.

VICTORIA. As long as I thought that poor Bill was dead I didn't want to forget him.

PATON. But why have you removed them both?

VICTORIA. I'm all at sea. I'm married to two men, and I feel as if I were married to neither.

PATON. I wish you weren't. I wish with all my heart you weren't.

VICTORIA. How emphatic you are. Why?

PATON. Can't you guess?

VICTORIA (*looking down*). I must be very stupid.

PATON. Don't you know that I dote upon you? I curse my unhappy fate that I didn't meet you before you were married.

VICTORIA (*rising*). Would you have asked me to marry you?

PATON (*rising*). Morning, noon and night until you consented.

VICTORIA (*easing* C.). I never want a Paris model so much as when I know it's just been sold to somebody else. I wonder if you'd want to marry me if I were free?

PATON. Yes. With all my heart.

VICTORIA. But I'm not free.

PATON. And you—if you were, would you marry me?

VICTORIA. Tell me, why do you wear spats?

PATON. I think they're so neat.

VICTORIA. Oh, not because you suffer from cold feet?

PATON. Oh no, my circulation is excellent.

VICTORIA. I don't believe you're the sort of man who'd ever take no for an answer.

PATON. You're perfectly adorable.

VICTORIA (*with a smile; shyly*). I wonder if you'd take me out to luncheon? (*She picks up* PATON's *hat and gloves*.)

PATON (*moving to* R. *of her*). Give me the chance.

VICTORIA (*handing the hat and gloves to him*). I'll just dress myself. Come back in half an hour, and you'll find me ready.

PATON. Very well.

VICTORIA. Good-bye for the present.

(VICTORIA *and* PATON *exit up* L. *After a few moments,* WILLIAM *is heard off up* L.)

WILLIAM (*off; calling*). Victoria.

(*He enters up* L. *He wears a different suit and slippers.*)

(*He calls.*) Hulloa! (*He shouts.*) Freddie!

FREDERICK (*off; calling*). Hulloa!

WILLIAM (*calling*). Freddie. (*He moves down* L.C.)

(FREDERICK *enters up* L. *He still wears his overcoat and carries the rug and newspaper.*)

I say, I can't find my shoes.

FREDERICK (*moving to the settee*). Your shoes? What do you want your shoes for? (*He puts the rug and paper on the settee.*)

WILLIAM. To put them on. What else d'you think I want them for?

FREDERICK. I saw them lying about. (*He moves into the bay and looks around.*) I thought I'd better put them away in case of accidents.

WILLIAM. Silly ass. Where did you put them?

FREDERICK (*looking in the gramophone*). I was just trying to think.

WILLIAM. You don't mean to say you don't know where they are?

FREDERICK. Of course I know where they are because I put them there, but I don't happen to remember just at the moment.

WILLIAM. Well, you hurry up and remember.

FREDERICK (*crossing to the fireplace*). Don't fuss me. I can't possibly remember if you fuss me.

WILLIAM (*moving* L. *of the settee*). Try and think where you put them.

FREDERICK (*looking doubtfully at a vase*). I know I didn't put them in one of the flower vases.

WILLIAM. So I should hope.

FREDERICK. They might be in the coal-scuttle.

WILLIAM. If they are I'll black your face with them.

FREDERICK (*looking in the scuttle; with triumph*). I said they weren't in the coal-scuttle.

WILLIAM. Fathead. I don't want to know where they're not. I want to know where they are.

FREDERICK. If I knew that I shouldn't be hunting for them.

WILLIAM. If you don't find them in two and a half seconds I'll break every bone in your body.

FREDERICK (*sitting on the settee*). It's no good losing your hair about it. If we can't find your shoes we can't. (*He wraps himself in the rug.*)

WILLIAM (*irritably*). I say, what the devil have you got all the windows open for?

FREDERICK. I was trying to warm the room a bit. Besides, they say it's healthy.

c

WILLIAM (*moving into the bay*). A short life and a merry one for me. I like a fug. (*He shuts the windows.*)

FREDERICK. That won't make it any warmer. I've tried that.

WILLIAM (*moving to the alcove up* L.). You silly ass, why don't you light the fire? (*He shuts the alcove window.*)

FREDERICK. Don't be so damned unpatriotic. Victoria must have a fire in her bedroom, and we must have one in the nursery.

WILLIAM. Why?

FREDERICK. For the children's bath.

WILLIAM (*astonished*). What, every day?

FREDERICK. Yes, they wash children a lot nowadays.

WILLIAM (*moving* C.). Poor little beggars.

(FREDERICK *suddenly throws off the rug and rises.*)

FREDERICK (*moving to* R. *of* WILLIAM). Where the devil did you get that suit?

WILLIAM. Rather saucy, I flatter myself. Victoria sent it in to me.

FREDERICK. She needn't have sent you the only new suit I've had since the war. Upon my soul, I think it's a bit thick.

WILLIAM. Well, you didn't like the suit I wore yesterday. You can't expect me to go about in fig-leaves unless you have the house properly warmed.

FREDERICK (*picking up the rug and crossing to the desk down* L.). If you'd had the decency to ask *me* you might have had this suit I've got on. (*He puts the rug on the desk chair.*)

WILLIAM. Thanks, but I don't altogether like that one. It's a bit baggy at the knees for me.

FREDERICK. You're very much mistaken if you think you're going to wear all the new clothes and I'm going to wear all the old ones.

WILLIAM (*moving to* R. *of* FREDERICK). If you're going to be shirty about it, where the devil did you get that pin?

FREDERICK. Oh, Victoria gave it me on my birthday.

WILLIAM. Well, it's mine. She gave it me on my birthday first. And where did you get those links?

FREDERICK. Victoria gave them to me as a Christmas present.

WILLIAM. Oh, did she? She gave them to me as a Christmas present before she gave them to you. You jolly well take them off.

FREDERICK. I'll see you blowed first. At your death you left everything to her in your will. If she chose to give them to me it's no business of yours.

WILLIAM (*moving to the fireplace*). Well, I'm not going to argue about it, but I think it's dashed bad form to swank about in a dead man's jewellery.

FREDERICK (*moving* C.). By the way, did you ever have a hammered gold cigarette-case?

WILLIAM. Rather. That was Victoria's wedding present to me. Did you get it, too?

FREDERICK. Thrifty woman, Victoria.

WILLIAM. I say, unless I have a fire I shall turn into the Albert Memorial.

FREDERICK. Apply a match and see what happens.

WILLIAM. Thanks—I will. (*He takes a box of matches from his pocket and lights the fire.*)

FREDERICK (*moving up* C.). Now I'll take my coat off. Victoria will be furious. (*He takes off his overcoat and puts it on the love-seat.*)

WILLIAM. That's your look out. You'll have to take the responsibility.

FREDERICK (*moving to the armchair* C.). It's got nothing to do with me. You're the master of this house.

WILLIAM. Not at all. I am but an honoured guest.

FREDERICK (*sitting in the armchair*). Oh no, the moment you appeared I sank into insignificance.

WILLIAM (*sitting on the settee*). My dear fellow, where did I sleep last night? In the spare bedroom. That proves conclusively that I am a guest and nothing more.

FREDERICK. And where the devil do you think I slept? Here.

WILLIAM. Why did you do that? You were perfectly sober when I went to bed.

FREDERICK. Victoria said I couldn't sleep in the next room to hers now you were back.

WILLIAM. Oh, well, I dare say you made yourself very comfortable on the sofa.

FREDERICK. Look at the damned thing.

WILLIAM. By the way, what's the matter with the furniture?

FREDERICK. When you were killed Victoria was naturally very much upset, so she had the drawing-room redecorated.

WILLIAM. I dare say I'm not very bright so early in the morning, but I don't quite see the connection.

FREDERICK. You see, the old room had too many painful associations. She wanted to distract her mind.

WILLIAM. Oh, I was under the impression that you'd undertaken that.

FREDERICK (*with dignity*). I was sympathetic. That is surely what you would have liked me to be.

WILLIAM. Of course. I'm not blaming you.

FREDERICK. If you'd seen Victoria in tears you couldn't expect a man not to try and console her.

WILLIAM. She's the only woman I ever knew who looks as pretty when she cries as when she smiles. It's a great power.

FREDERICK. I knew you'd take it like a sensible man.

WILLIAM. Quite so.

FREDERICK. When would you like me to clear out?

WILLIAM. My dear fellow, why should you wish to do that?

Surely you don't for a moment imagine that I shall be in the way. I propose to make my visit quite a brief one.

FREDERICK. I'm sorry to hear that. Victoria will be disappointed. But of course that's no concern of mine. You and your wife must arrange that between you.

WILLIAM. My dear old thing, you entirely misunderstand me. I am not the man to come between husband and wife.

FREDERICK (*rising*). What the devil do you mean?

WILLIAM (*rising*). Well, if it comes to that, what the devil do you mean?

(VICTORIA *enters up* L. *She now wears a most becoming morning dress. She carries a box of chocolates.*)

VICTORIA (*to* WILLIAM). Good morning. (*She moves to* WILLIAM *and gives him her right cheek to kiss.*)

WILLIAM. Good morning. (*He kisses* VICTORIA.)

VICTORIA (*to* FREDERICK). Good morning. (*She moves to* FREDERICK *and gives him her left cheek to kiss.*)

FREDERICK. Good morning. (*He kisses* VICTORIA.)

VICTORIA (*with a nod of the head towards* WILLIAM). I went to him first because he's been away so long.

FREDERICK. Naturally. And he was your husband long before I was.

VICTORIA (*between* WILLIAM *and* FREDERICK). I don't want either of you to be jealous of the other. I adore you both and I'm not going to show any favouritism.

FREDERICK. I don't see why he should have the spare bedroom, while I have to double up on the drawing-room sofa.

WILLIAM. I like that. What about the fatted calf?

FREDERICK. Not unless you've brought your coupons with you.

VICTORIA (*catching sight of the fire*). Who lit that fire?

FREDERICK. He did.

WILLIAM. It was his match.

(VICTORIA *crosses to the chair down* R., *draws it up and sits in front of the fire in such a way as to prevent any warmth from getting into the room.*)

VICTORIA (*eating a chocolate*). Of course you don't care if we run so short of coal that my wretched babies die of double pneumonia. It's simply criminal to have a fire here.

WILLIAM. I'm tortured by the pangs of remorse. But, need you monopolize it?

VICTORIA. If there is a fire I may as well get some benefit out of it.

FREDERICK. Are those chocolates you're eating, Victoria?

VICTORIA. Yes, Bobbie Curtis sent them to me. They're delicious.

FREDERICK. Are they?

VICTORIA. It's so hard to get good chocolates just now.

FREDERICK. I know it is. I haven't tasted one for months.

VICTORIA (*biting a chocolate*). Oh, this one's soft inside. How hateful. Would either of you like it?

(FREDERICK *crosses quickly towards* VICTORIA.)

WILLIAM (*ironically*). It seems a pity to waste it, Victoria. (*He holds* FREDERICK *away and attempts to get the chocolate himself.*)

VICTORIA (*eating the chocolate*). I dare say you're right. One oughtn't to be too particular in war time.

(FREDERICK *turns and eases* c.)

WILLIAM. Ah, I suppose that's what you thought when you married Freddie.

VICTORIA. I did that for your sake, darling. He was such a pal of yours.

FREDERICK. She was simply inconsolable when you were killed.

WILLIAM (*easing* L. *of the settee*). It's lucky you were there to console her.

VICTORIA. It was Freddie who broke the news to me. He thought of the memorial service. He came to see me twice a day.

WILLIAM. And with your practical mind I suppose you thought it hardly worth his while to wear out shoe-leather when a trifling ceremony might save him the journey.

VICTORIA. Of course we waited the year. I told him he mustn't think of it till the year was up.

WILLIAM. With leather so expensive? But you always had nice feelings, Victoria.

VICTORIA (*rising and turning*). You know how helpless I am without a man. I knew you wouldn't wish me to remain a widow.

FREDERICK. I felt I was the proper person to look after her.

WILLIAM. The way you've both of you sacrificed yourselves for my sake is almost more than I can bear. I can only hope that you didn't have to force your inclinations too much?

FREDERICK. What do you mean by that?

WILLIAM. Well, since it appears you married entirely for my sake, I presume there was nothing between you but—shall we say esteem?

VICTORIA. Oh, but, Bill darling, didn't I tell you that I adored Freddie? It was his wonderful friendship for you that won my heart.

FREDERICK. She was so devoted to you, Bill, I should have been a brute not to care for her.

WILLIAM. One would almost think you fell in love with one another.

VICTORIA (*turning to face the fire*). Only over your dead body, darling.

FREDERICK. I should have thought you'd be rather touched by it.

WILLIAM. It gives me quite a lump in my throat.

FREDERICK. And Victoria never forgot you, old man. Did you, Victoria?

VICTORIA. Never. (*She puts the box of chocolates on the table* R. *of the settee, then replaces the chair in its original position down* R.)

FREDERICK. I know quite well that I only came second in her heart. So long as you were round and about she would never have thought of me.

WILLIAM. Oh, I don't know about that. Even the most constant woman likes a change now and then.

FREDERICK. No, no. I know Victoria's faithful heart. She can never really love any man but you. Victoria, you know how I adore you. You are the only woman in the world for me. But I realize that there is only one thing for me to do. Bill has come back. There is only one course open to me as a gentleman and a man of honour. It is a bitter, bitter sacrifice, but I am equal to it. I renounce all rights in you. I will go away, a wiser and a sadder man, and leave you to Bill. (*He crosses to* VICTORIA.) Good-bye, Victoria. Wipe your mouth and give me one more kiss before we part for ever.

(WILLIAM *moves quickly to the alcove steps.*)

VICTORIA. Oh, how beautiful of you, Freddie. What a soul you've got.

(*They embrace and kiss.*)

FREDERICK. Good-bye, Victoria. Forget me and live happily with a better man than I.

VICTORIA. I shall never forget you, Freddie. Good-bye. Go quickly or I shall break down.

(WILLIAM *plants himself firmly in front of the steps.* FREDERICK *goes up to him with outstretched hand.*)

FREDERICK. Good-bye, Bill. Be kind to her. I couldn't do this for anyone but you.

WILLIAM (*deliberately*). Nothing doing.

FREDERICK. I am going out of your life for ever.

WILLIAM. Not in those boots.

FREDERICK. Damn it all, what's the matter with them? They're not yours.

WILLIAM. A figure of speech, my lad.

FREDERICK. I don't think this is exactly the moment for flippancy. You get away from those steps.

WILLIAM. You shall only pass over my dead body.

FREDERICK. What's the good of that? I shouldn't get the chance then.

VICTORIA (*moving* C.). Bill, why prolong a painful scene?

WILLIAM. My dear Victoria, I am not the man to accept a sacrifice like that. No, I will not come between you.

VICTORIA. Oh, Bill, how noble.

WILLIAM. Victoria, I am a gentleman and a soldier. This being that you see before you, notwithstanding the tolerable suit he wears, is a disembodied wraith. To all intents and purposes I am as dead as mutton. I will remain so.

FREDERICK. Victoria will never be happy with me now that you've come back.

WILLIAM. Not another word. She is yours.

FREDERICK (*turning and moving down* R.). My dear Bill, you know me very little. I am lazy, selfish, bad-tempered, mean, gouty, and predisposed to cancer, tuberculosis, and diabetes.

WILLIAM. This is terrible, my poor Freddie. You must take the greatest care of your health and dear Victoria will do her best to correct your defects of character.

FREDERICK. If you really loved her you wouldn't expose her to the certain misery that it must be to live with a man like me.

WILLIAM (*easing down* L.C.). Freddie, old man, I can no longer conceal from you that with a constitution ruined by dissipation in my youth and broken by the ravages of war I have not much longer to live. Besides, Victoria knows only too well that I am vindictive and overbearing, extravagant, violent, and mendacious.

VICTORIA. I understand it all. You're both so noble. You're both so heroic. You're both so unselfish.

(TAYLOR *enters up* L. *She carries a slip of paper.*)

TAYLOR (*moving to* L. *of* VICTORIA). If you please, ma'am, someone to see you from the Alexandra Employment Agency. (*She hands her the slip of paper.*)

VICTORIA (*after a glance*). Oh, send her in at once.

TAYLOR. Very good, madam.

(*She exits up* L.)

VICTORIA. A cook. A cook. A cook.

FREDERICK (*sitting on the settee at the* R. *end of it*). Good business. Is she plain or good?

VICTORIA. Plain and good.

WILLIAM (*crossing to the settee*). How like a woman. (*He sits* L. *of* FREDERICK *on the settee.*)

(TAYLOR *enters up* L. *and shows in* MRS POGSON, *who is large, heavy and authoritative. She is dressed like the widow of an undertaker and carries a large black handbag.* TAYLOR *exits up* L.)

MRS POGSON (*on the alcove steps*). Good morning.

VICTORIA. Good morning.

(MRS POGSON *moves down* L.C.)

WILLIAM ⎫
FREDERICK ⎰ (*together*). Good morning.

(MRS POGSON *puts her handbag on the table* C. *and sits in the armchair.*)

MRS POGSON. I 'ave your name on the list the Alexandra gave me as requiring a cook. I don't know as I very much like this neighbourhood, but I thought I'd just pop in and see if the position looked like suiting me.

VICTORIA (*ingratiatingly*). I'm sure you'd find it a very nice one.

MRS POGSON. Why did the last cook leave you?

VICTORIA. She was going to be married.

MRS POGSON. Ah, that's what all you ladies say. Of course, it may be so, and on the other 'and it may not.

VICTORIA. She told me she hadn't had a nicer place for the last three months.

MRS POGSON. Now before we go any further I'd just like to know one thing. Have you got a garage?

VICTORIA. Well, we have, but there are no cars in it. We sold our car.

MRS POGSON. Oh, well, that would be very convenient. I always bring my Ford with me.

VICTORIA. Yes, of course.

MRS POGSON. Do you keep men-servants?

VICTORIA. No, I'm afraid not.

MRS POGSON (*severely*). I've always been used to men-servants.

VICTORIA. You see, since the war . . .

MRS POGSON. Oh, you don't 'ave to tell me. I know it's very difficult. Of course, I leave you to make any arrangements you like about lighting the kitchen fire. All I ask is that it should be alight when I come down in the morning.

VICTORIA. Oh! But I don't quite know how I should manage about that.

MRS POGSON. In my last position the gentleman of the house lit the fire every morning.

VICTORIA (*glancing at* WILLIAM *and* FREDERICK). Oh, I hadn't thought of that.

WILLIAM. I wouldn't if I were you, Victoria.

MRS POGSON. A very nice gentleman he was too. Brought me up a cup of tea and a slice of thin bread and butter every day before I got up.

VICTORIA. I'm sure we'd do everything we could to make you comfortable.

MRS POGSON. What cooking would you require?

VICTORIA. Of course, I know it's very difficult to have a great variety now. I'm sure you'll do the best you can. We're out for luncheon a good deal and we dine at eight.

MRS POGSON. Of course, you can please yourselves there, but I never do any cooking after middle-day.

VICTORIA. That's rather awkward.

MRS POGSON (*picking up her handbag*). If you don't think I'll suit you I needn't waste any more of my time. I've got ten to a dozen ladies that I must interview this morning.

VICTORIA (*hastily*). Oh, I wouldn't make a point of that. I dare say we can arrange our hours to suit you.

MRS POGSON (*replacing her handbag on the table*). Well, I always serve up my dinner at one o'clock. A nice little bit of meat and a milk pudding.

VICTORIA. I see. And what—what wages are you asking?

MRS POGSON. I don't know as I'm asking any wages. I'm prepared to accept a salary of two pounds a week.

VICTORIA. That's rather more than I've been in the habit of paying.

MRS POGSON (*rising*). If you aren't prepared to pay that, there are plenty as are. (*She picks up her handbag.*)

VICTORIA. We won't quarrel about that. I'm sure you're worth the money.

MRS POGSON. There, I was just going away and I knew I 'ad one more question to ask you. How many are you in the family?

VICTORIA. Well, I have two children, but they give no trouble at all, and just at present they're not staying here.

MRS POGSON. Oh, I don't mind children. I've had too many meself to do that.

VICTORIA. And then there's just me and these two gentlemen.

MRS POGSON. I suppose you are married to one of them.

VICTORIA. I don't know what you mean by that. I'm married to both.

MRS POGSON. Both? Legally?

VICTORIA (*moving above the settee*). Of course. (*She stands behind the settee with her left hand on* WILLIAM'S *left shoulder and her right hand on* FREDERICK'S *right shoulder.*)

MRS POGSON. Well, I do call that going it. (*With growing indignation.*) If it 'ad been just a gentleman friend I'd 'ave 'ad nothing to say. I've lived in the very best families and I'm quite used to that. It keeps the lady quiet and good-tempered and she ain't always fussing about one thing and another. And if he lives in the 'ouse she ain't likely to keep the dinner waiting for 'alf an hour every other day. But if you're married to 'im that's quite another thing. It's not justice. If you ladies think you're going to 'ave two 'usbands while many a working woman can't even get one—well, all I say is, it's not justice. I've bin a Conservative all me life, but thank God I've got a vote now, and I tell you straight what I'm going to do, I'm going to vote Labour. (*She moves up* L. *and turns.*) Disgusting!

(*She flaunts out up* L.)

WILLIAM. Bang!

VICTORIA (*furiously*). The position is intolerable. I must have one husband. There are all sorts of ways in which a husband is indispensable. But only one. I cannot and will not have two.

FREDERICK. I have an idea.

WILLIAM. It's sure to be a rotten one.

FREDERICK. Let's draw lots.

WILLIAM. I knew it was a rotten one.

VICTORIA (*moving to* L. *of the settee*). How d'you mean, Freddie?

FREDERICK. Well, we'll take two pieces of paper and make a cross on one of them. Then we'll fold them up and put them in a hat. We'll draw, and the one who draws the cross gets Victoria.

VICTORIA (*mollified*). That'll be rather thrilling.

WILLIAM. I'd sooner toss for it. I'm lucky at tossing.

FREDERICK. Do you mean to say you funk it?

WILLIAM. I don't exactly funk it. It's an awful risk to take.

VICTORIA (*easing* C.). It'll be so romantic. Get some paper, Freddie.

FREDERICK (*rising*). All right. (*He crosses to the desk down* L.)

WILLIAM (*worried*). I don't like it. This isn't my lucky day. I saw the new moon through glass. I knew something was going wrong the moment I opened my egg this morning.

(FREDERICK *takes two small pieces of paper from the desk drawer and with his back to the others draws a cross on both pieces and folds them up.*)

FREDERICK (*turning*). Whoever draws the blank paper renounces all claim to Victoria. He vanishes from the scene like a puff of smoke. He will never be heard of again.

WILLIAM (*rising*). I don't like it. I repeat that I only do it under protest.

VICTORIA. Now, Bill, don't be disagreeable the moment you come back.

FREDERICK. You'll have plenty of time for that during the next forty years.

VICTORIA. You seem rather above yourself, Freddie. Supposing *you* draw the blank?

FREDERICK. I saw a dappled horse this morning. (*He looks around.*) What shall we put them in.

VICTORIA. The waste-paper basket is the best thing.

FREDERICK (*picking up the waste-paper basket*). Right! Now you quite understand. (*He puts the papers in the basket.*) One of these papers has a cross on it. I will put the two papers in the basket, and Victoria shall hold it. It is agreed that whoever draws a blank shall leave the house at once.

WILLIAM (*faintly*). Yes.

FREDERICK (*handing* VICTORIA *the basket*). Here you are. Victoria.

WILLIAM (*with agitation*). Shake 'em well.

VICTORIA. All right. (*She shakes the basket.*) I say, isn't this thrilling?

FREDERICK. You draw first, Bill.

(VICTORIA *offers the basket to* WILLIAM.)

WILLIAM (*shaking like a leaf*). No, I can't. I really can't.

FREDERICK. It's your right. You are Victoria's first husband.

VICTORIA. He's right there, Bill. You must have the first dip in the lucky bag.

WILLIAM. This is awful. I'm sweating like a pig.

VICTORIA. It's too exciting. My heart is simply going pit-a-pat. I wonder which of you will get me.

WILLIAM (*hesitating*). Going over the top is nothing to it.

FREDERICK. Courage, old man, courage.

WILLIAM. It's no good, I can't. You must remember that my nerves are all to pieces after three years in a German prison.

VICTORIA. I see how much you love me, Bill.

FREDERICK. Shut your eyes, man, and make a plunge for the basket.

WILLIAM. The only thing is to get it over. I wish I'd been a better man. (*He draws one of the papers from the basket. For a moment, he looks at it nervously, unable to bring himself to unfold it.*)

(VICTORIA *offers the basket to* FREDERICK *who draws the other paper. He quickly opens it, starts back and gives a sudden cry.*)

FREDERICK (*breaking down* L.; *dramatically*). Blank. Blank. Blank. (*He puts the paper in his pocket.*)

(WILLIAM *gives a start and quickly opens the paper in his hand. He stares at it in horror.* VICTORIA *puts the basket on the table* C.)

WILLIAM (*sitting on the settee*). My God!

VICTORIA (*moving to* FREDERICK). Oh, my poor Freddie!

FREDERICK (*leaning on the desk chair with his back to* VICTORIA; *with enormous feeling*). Don't pity me, Victoria. I want all my courage now. I've lost you and I must bid you good-bye for ever.

VICTORIA. Oh, Freddie, this is too dreadful! You must come and see me from time to time.

FREDERICK. I couldn't. That is more than I could bear. (*He turns.*) I shall never forget you. You are the only woman I have ever loved.

(*At these words* WILLIAM *looks up and observes* FREDERICK *curiously.*)

VICTORIA. You'll never love another, will you? I shouldn't like that.

(WILLIAM *rises.*)

FREDERICK. How could I love anyone after you? Why, you might as well ask a man to see when the sun has gone down.

WILLIAM. He can turn on the electric light, you know.

FREDERICK. Ah, you can jest. I am a broken-hearted and a ruined man.

WILLIAM. I was only suggesting the possibility of consolation.

VICTORIA (*turning and moving to* L. *of* WILLIAM). I don't think that's very nice of you, Bill. I thought what he said extremely poetic. Besides, I don't want him to be consoled.

FREDERICK (*moving to* L. *of* VICTORIA). Give me one last kiss, Victoria.

VICTORIA. Darling!

(FREDERICK *seizes her in his arms and kisses her.*)

FREDERICK (*the hero of romance*). Good-bye. I go into the night.

WILLIAM. Oh, aren't you going at once?

FREDERICK. I am.

WILLIAM (*moving above the others to the alcove steps*). Well, it happens to be the middle of the day.

FREDERICK (*with dignity*). I was speaking in metaphor.

WILLIAM. Before you go you might just let me have a look at that other bit of paper, the one with the blank on it.

FREDERICK (*moving up* L.). Oh, don't delay me with foolish trifling.

WILLIAM (*intercepting him*). I'm sorry to detain you.

FREDERICK (*trying to dodge round him*). Why d'you want to see it?

WILLIAM (*preventing him*). Mere curiosity.

FREDERICK (*trying the other side*). Really, Bill, I don't know how you can be so heartless as to give way to curiosity when my heart is one great aching wound.

WILLIAM. I should like to have the two pieces framed, an interesting souvenir of an important occasion.

FREDERICK. Any other piece will do just as well. I threw that one in the fire.

WILLIAM. Oh no, you didn't. You put it in your pocket.

FREDERICK. I've had enough of this. Can't you see that I'm a desperate man?

WILLIAM. Not half so desperate as I am. If you don't give me that bit of paper quietly I'll take it from you.

FREDERICK (*turning and moving down* R.). Go to blazes!

WILLIAM (*quickly following* FREDERICK). Give it up.

(*During the ensuing lines* FREDERICK *jumps over the settee and dodges behind the love-seat.* WILLIAM *follows over the settee and chases after* FREDERICK.)

VICTORIA. What's the matter? (*She moves quickly down* L.C.) Have you both gone mad?

WILLIAM (*to* FREDERICK). You'll have to sooner or later.

FREDERICK. I'll see you damned first.

VICTORIA. Why don't you give it him?

FREDERICK (*above the love-seat*). Not if I know it.

VICTORIA. Why not?

FREDERICK. I won't have my feelings hurt like this.

WILLIAM (*below the love-seat*). I'll hurt a lot more than your feelings in a minute.

(FREDERICK *makes a sudden bolt up* L., *but* WILLIAM *catches him.*)

Gotcher. Now will you give it up? (*He twists* FREDERICK'S *arm behind his back and pushes him* C.)

FREDERICK. Not on your life.

WILLIAM. I'll break your bally arm if you don't.

FREDERICK (*writing*). Oh, you devil! Stop it. You're hurting me.

WILLIAM. I'm trying to.

FREDERICK. Hit him on the head with the poker, Victoria.

WILLIAM. Don't be unlady-like, Victoria.

FREDERICK. You filthy Boche. All right, here it is.

(WILLIAM *lets him go and* FREDERICK *takes the paper out of his pocket. Just as* WILLIAM *thinks he is going to give it him, he puts it in his mouth.*)

WILLIAM (*seizing him by the throat*). Take it out of your mouth.

(FREDERICK *takes the paper out and throws it on to the floor.*)

FREDERICK (*moving to the fireplace*). I don't know if you call yourself a gentleman.

(WILLIAM *picks up the paper and unfolds it.*)

WILLIAM. You dirty dog.

VICTORIA. What's the matter?

WILLIAM (*moving to* VICTORIA). Look. (*He shows her the paper.*)

VICTORIA. Why, it's got a cross on it.

WILLIAM (*indignantly*). They both had crosses on them.

VICTORIA. I don't understand.

WILLIAM. Don't you? He was making quite sure that *I* shouldn't draw a blank.

(VICTORIA *looks at* WILLIAM *in astonishment. There is a moment's pause.*)

FREDERICK (*magnanimously*). I did it for your sake, Victoria. I knew that your heart was set on Bill, only you couldn't bear to hurt my feelings, so I thought I'd make it easier for you.

VICTORIA (*crossing to* FREDERICK). That was just like you, Freddie. You have a charming nature.

WILLIAM (*acidly*). It almost brings tears to my eyes.

FREDERICK. I'm made that way. I can't help sacrificing myself for others.

(TAYLOR *enters up* L.)

TAYLOR. May I speak to you for a minute, madam.

VICTORIA. Not now. I'm busy.

TAYLOR. I'm afraid it's very urgent, madam.

VICTORIA (*moving up* L.C.). Oh, very well, I'll come. (*She turns. To* WILLIAM *and* FREDERICK.) Don't say anything important till I come back.

(*She exits up* L. TAYLOR *follows her off.*)

FREDERICK. How did you guess?

WILLIAM (*moving to the love-seat*). You were so devilish calm about it.

FREDERICK (*moving to the table* C., *picking up the basket and replacing it above the desk*). That was the calm of despair.

(WILLIAM *sits on the love-seat and hurriedly rises again. He turns, feels under the cushion and draws out a pair of shoes.*)

WILLIAM. My shoes!

FREDERICK (*moving* C.). I knew I'd put them somewhere.

WILLIAM. You didn't put them anywhere. You hid them, you dirty dog.

FREDERICK. It's a lie. Why the dickens should I hide your rotten old boots?

WILLIAM (*moving to the fireplace*). You were afraid I'd do a bunk. (*He puts the shoes to warm in the hearth.*)

FREDERICK. You needn't get ratty about it. I only ascribed to you the disinterested motives that I—that I have myself. I may be wrong, but, after all, it's a noble error.

WILLIAM (*turning to face him*). One might almost think you didn't want Victoria.

(FREDERICK *looks at* WILLIAM *for a moment thoughtfully, then he makes up his mind to make a clean breast of it.*)

FREDERICK (*moving* R.C.). Bill, old chap, you know I'm not the sort of man to say a word against my wife.

WILLIAM. Nor am I the sort of man to listen to a word against mine.

FREDERICK (*turning and moving* L.C.). But, hang it all, if a fellow can't discuss his wife dispassionately with her first husband, who can he discuss her with?

WILLIAM. I can't imagine unless it's with her second.

FREDERICK (*turning*). Tell me what you really think of Victoria.

WILLIAM. She's the sweetest little woman in the world.

FREDERICK. No man could want a better wife.

WILLIAM. She's pretty.

FREDERICK. Charming.

WILLIAM. Delightful.

FREDERICK (*sitting in the armchair*). I confess that sometimes I've thought it hard that when I wanted a thing it was selfishness, and when she wanted it, it was only her due.

WILLIAM (*sitting on the settee*). I don't mind admitting that sometimes I used to wonder why it was only natural of me to sacrifice my inclinations, but in her, the proof of a beautiful nature.

FREDERICK. It has tried me now and then that in every difference of opinion I should always be wrong and she should always be right.

WILLIAM. Sometimes I couldn't quite understand why my engagements were made to be broken, while nothing in the world must interfere with hers.

FREDERICK. I have asked myself occasionally why my time was of no importance while hers was so precious.

WILLIAM. I did sometimes wish I could call my soul my own.

FREDERICK. The fact is, I'm not worthy of her, Bill. As you so justly say, no man could want a better wife . . .

WILLIAM (*interrupting*). No, you said that.

FREDERICK. But I'm fed up. If you'd been dead I'd have seen it through like a gentleman, but you've turned up like a bad shilling. Now you take up the white man's burden.

WILLIAM (*rising and moving up* C.). I'll see you damned first.

FREDERICK. She must have one husband.

WILLIAM. Look here, there's only one thing to do. She must choose between us.

FREDERICK. That's not giving me a chance.

WILLIAM. I don't know what you mean by that. I think it's extraordinarily magnanimous on my part.

FREDERICK. Magnanimous be hanged. I've got a charming nature and I'm extremely handsome. Victoria will naturally choose me.

WILLIAM. Heaven knows I'm not vain, but I've always been given to understand that I'm an almost perfect specimen of manly beauty. (*He sits on the love-seat.*) My conversation is not only amusing but instructive.

FREDERICK. I'd rather toss for it.

WILLIAM. I'm not going to risk anything like that. I've had enough of your hanky-panky.

FREDERICK. I thought I was dealing with a gentleman.

WILLIAM. Here she comes.

(VICTORIA *enters up* L. *She is in a temper. She wears her hat and carries her gloves and handbag.* FREDERICK *and* WILLIAM *rise.*)

VICTORIA. All the servants have given notice now.

FREDERICK. They haven't!

VICTORIA (*moving above the table* C.). I've done everything in the world for them. I've fed them on the fat of the land. I've given them my own butter and my own sugar to eat.

FREDERICK. Only because they were bad for your figure, Victoria.

VICTORIA (*putting her gloves and bag on the table* c.). They didn't know that. (*She crosses to the fireplace.*) I've given them all the evenings out that I really didn't want them. (*She looks at herself in the mirror.*) I've let them bring the whole British Army to tea here. And now they give me notice.

WILLIAM (*moving to* R. *of* FREDERICK). It's a bit thick, I must say.

VICTORIA (*turning*). I argued with them, I appealed to them, I practically went down on my knees to them. They wouldn't listen. They're going to walk out of the house this afternoon.

WILLIAM. Oh, well, Freddie and I will do the housework until you get some more.

VICTORIA (*moving* R.C.). Do you know that it's harder to get a parlour-maid than a peerage? Why, every day at Paddington Registry Office you'll see a queue of old bachelors taking out licences to marry their cooks. (*She turns again to the mirror.*) It's the only way to keep them.

WILLIAM (*to* FREDERICK). Now?

FREDERICK (*to* WILLIAM). Yes.

WILLIAM. Well, Victoria, we've decided that there's only one thing to be done. You must choose between us.

VICTORIA (*turning*). How can I? I adore you both. Besides, there is nothing to choose between you.

WILLIAM. Oh, I don't know about that. Freddie has a charming nature and he's extremely handsome.

FREDERICK. I wish you wouldn't say that, Bill. Heaven knows you're not vain, but I must tell you to your face that you're an almost perfect specimen of manly beauty, and your conversation is not only amusing but instructive.

VICTORIA. I don't want to hurt anybody's feelings.

FREDERICK (*crossing below* WILLIAM *to* R.C.). Before you decide, I feel it only fair to make a confession to you. I could not bear it if our future life were founded on a lie. Victoria, in my department there is a stenographer. She is of the feminine gender. She has blue eyes and little yellow curls at the nape of her neck. The rest I leave to your imagination.

VICTORIA. How abominable. And I always thought you had such a nice mind.

FREDERICK. I am unworthy of you. I know it only too, too well. You can never forgive me. (*He turns and grins at* WILLIAM.)

WILLIAM. Dirty dog.

VICTORIA. That certainly simplifies matters. I don't quite see myself as the third lady in the back row of a harem.

WILLIAM. You would run no risk of being that in Canada. Women are scarce in Manitoba.

VICTORIA. What *are* you talking about?

WILLIAM (*crossing below* FREDERICK *to* R. *of him*). I have come to the conclusion that England offers me no future now the war is over. I shall resign my commission. The empire needs workers, and I am ready to take my part in reconstruction. Make me the happiest of men, Victoria, and we'll emigrate together.

(FREDERICK *eases down* L.C.)

VICTORIA. To Canada?

FREDERICK. Where the sables come from.

VICTORIA. Not the best ones.

WILLIAM. I shall buy a farm. I think it would be a very good plan if you employed your leisure in learning how to cook the simple fare on which we shall live. I believe you can wash?

VICTORIA (*with asperity*). Lace.

WILLIAM. But I think you should also learn how to milk cows.

VICTORIA. I don't like cows.

WILLIAM. I see the idea appeals to you. It will be a wonderful life, Victoria. You'll light the fire and scrub the floors, and you'll cook the dinner and wash the clothes. You'll vote.

VICTORIA. And what shall I do in my spare moments?

WILLIAM. We will cultivate your mind by reading the *Encyclopaedia Britannica* together. Take a good look at us, Victoria, and say which of us it's to be. (*He turns and grins at* FREDERICK.)

VICTORIA. To tell you the truth, I don't see why it should be either.

(WILLIAM *moves to* R. *of* FREDERICK.)

FREDERICK. Hang it all, it must be one or the other.

VICTORIA (*moving to the table* C. *and picking up her gloves*). I think no-one can deny that since the day I married you I've sacrificed myself in every mortal way. I've worked myself to the bone to make you comfortable. Very few men have ever had such a wife as I've been to both of you! But one must think of oneself sometimes. (*She puts on her gloves.*)

WILLIAM. How true.

VICTORIA (*moving to the fireplace*). The war is over now, and I think I've done my bit. I've married two D.S.O.'s. Now I want to marry a Rolls-Royce.

FREDERICK (*astonished*). But I thought you adored us.

VICTORIA. Well, you see, I adore you both. It's six of one and half a dozen of the other, and the result is . . .

WILLIAM. A wash-out.

FREDERICK. Hang it all, I think it's a bit thick. (*He puts his arm around* WILLIAM'S *shoulders*.) Do you mean to say that you've fixed up to marry somebody else behind our back?

VICTORIA. You know I wouldn't do a thing like that, Freddie.

FREDERICK. Well, I don't tumble.

D

VICTORIA. My dear Freddie, have you ever studied the domestic habits of the unicorn?

FREDERICK. We're afraid our education was very much neglected.

VICTORIA (*moving to the table* C. *and picking up her handbag*). The unicorn is a shy and somewhat timid animal, and it is impossible to catch him with the snares of the hunter. But he is strangely impressionable to the charms of the fair sex. When he hears the frou-frou of a silk petticoat he forgets his native caution. In short, a pretty woman can lead him by the nose.

(TAYLOR *enters up* L.)

TAYLOR. Mr Leicester Paton is downstairs in his car, madam.
VICTORIA. Is it the Rolls-Royce?
TAYLOR. I think it is, madam.
VICTORIA (*with a smile of triumph*). Say I'll come down at once.
TAYLOR. Very good, madam.

(*She exits up* L.)

VICTORIA. The unicorn's going to take me out to luncheon.
She makes a long nose at them and exits up L. *as—*

the CURTAIN *falls.*

ACT III

SCENE.—*The kitchen. Noon, the next day.*

The kitchen is in the basement and is large, clean, sanitary and cheerful. The tradesmen's entrance is up C. *and opens on to the area.* L. *of the door there are two iron-barred windows through which the area steps leading up to the street can be seen. Anyone ascending or descending the steps is visible to the audience. Access to the ground floor of the house is by a small staircase of which the last few steps are visible, up* R. *The sink, draining-board and a small cupboard are under the windows. There is a large dresser against the wall* L. *A kitchen range, with a gas-stove above it, stands in a recess* R. *A large kitchen table stands* C. *with two chairs above it and one each* R. *and* L. *of it. There are other chairs* R. *of the door up* C. *and above the dresser. The kitchen is well appointed with the usual pots, pans, china, etc. There is a large electric bell and indicator board on the wall* R. *The floor is covered with linoleum.*

(See the Ground Plan at the end of the Play.)

When the CURTAIN *rises* WILLIAM, *in his shirt-sleeves is seated* L. *of the table. He has his feet up on it and reads a thin paper-bound novel of the sort that is published at threepence and sold by the newsagent round the corner. There is a pile of dirty crockery and pans on the draining board. The range fire is lit and a piece of steak is frying in a pan on top of it. A saucepan of potatoes is boiling on the gas-stove. The bell is ringing furiously.* FREDERICK *enters up* C. *He carries a scuttle of coal. Both* FREDERICK *and* WILLIAM *wear aprons.*

FREDERICK (*looking up at the bell*). Wait! (*He puts the scuttle down on the floor above the steps up* R.) I say, these coals weigh about a ton.

(The bell stops.)

You might carry them upstairs.

WILLIAM (*cheerfully*). I might, but I'm not going to.

FREDERICK. I wouldn't ask you, only since I was wounded in the arm serving my country, I haven't the strength I had once.

WILLIAM (*suspiciously*). Which arm were you wounded in?

FREDERICK (*promptly*). Both arms.

WILLIAM. Carry the coals on your head, then. I believe that's the best way really. And they said it improves the figure.

FREDERICK (*moving to the cupboard up* C.). You heartless devil. (*He gets* VICTORIA's *shoes and the polisher from the cupboard up* C. *and puts them on the* R. *end of the table.*)

WILLIAM. I'd do it like a shot, old man, only the doctor said it was very bad for my heart to carry heavy weights.

FREDERICK. What's the matter with your heart? You said you were wounded in the head.

WILLIAM. Besides, it isn't my work. I'm doing the cooking. You really can't expect me to do housework as well.

FREDERICK (*sitting* R. *of the table*). *Are* you doing the cooking? It looks to me as though you were just sitting about doing nothing. I don't see why I should have to sweat my life out. (*He polishes the shoes.*)

WILLIAM. You see, you have no organization. Housework's perfectly simple, only you must have organization. I have organization. That's my secret.

FREDERICK. I was a mug to say I'd do the housework. I might have known you'd freeze on to a soft job if there was one.

WILLIAM. I naturally undertook to do what I could do best. That is one of the secrets of organization. Cooking is an art. Any fool can do housework.

FREDERICK. I'll give you a thick ear in a minute. You just try and get a shine on a pair of shoes and see if it's easy.

WILLIAM. I don't believe you know how to shine a pair of shoes. Did you spit on them?

FREDERICK (*rising*). No, only on the silver. (*He replaces the polisher in the cupboard and puts the shoes on the floor by the coal scuttle.*)

WILLIAM. You just look nippy and get the table laid while I finish my book.

FREDERICK (*gloomily*). Is it luncheon or dinner? (*He moves to the dresser and gets a tablecloth from the drawer.*)

WILLIAM. I don't know yet, but we're going to have it down here because it's easier for dishing up. Organization again.

FREDERICK (*moving to* R. *of the table*). What does Victoria say to that?

WILLIAM. I haven't told her yet.

FREDERICK. She's in an awful temper this morning.

WILLIAM. Why?

FREDERICK (*shaking out the cloth over the table*). Because the water in the bathroom wasn't hot. (*The far end of the cloth drapes itself over* WILLIAM's *feet.*)

WILLIAM. Wasn't it?

FREDERICK (*moving above the* L. *end of the table*). You know very well it wasn't. (*He tries to settle the cloth.*)

WILLIAM. I think cold baths are much better for people. There'd be a damned sight less illness about if cold baths were compulsory.

FREDERICK. Tell that to the horse-marines. (*He pushes* WILLIAM's *feet off the table.*) You were too lazy to get up in time. That's all there is to it. (*He adjusts the cloth.*)

WILLIAM. I wish you'd get on with your work instead of interrupting me all the time.

FREDERICK. You don't look as if you were so busy as all that. (*He peers over* WILLIAM's *shoulder at the novel.*)

WILLIAM. I want to find out if the nursery governess married the duke after all. You should read this after I've finished it.

FREDERICK (*moving to the dresser*). I don't have time for reading. (*He picks up the cutlery-basket.*) When I take on a job I like to do it properly. (*He moves above the table.*)

WILLIAM. I wish you wouldn't mumble.

FREDERICK (*banging the basket onto the table in front of* WILLIAM). What is there for lunch? (*He moves to the gas-stove and takes the lid off the saucepan.*) What's this mess?

WILLIAM. Those are potatoes. (*He takes a fork from the basket and waves it.*) You might give one of them a jab with a fork to see how they're getting on.

FREDERICK (*moving to* WILLIAM). It seems rather unfriendly, doesn't it?

WILLIAM (*giving* FREDERICK *the fork*). Oh no, they're used to it.

(FREDERICK *takes the fork, moves to the gas-stove, and tries to transfix a potato.*)

FREDERICK. Damn it all, they won't stop still. They're wriggling all over the place. Wriggle, wriggle, little tater. How I wonder who's your mater. Poetry! Come here, you little devil. Woa there.

WILLIAM. I say, don't make such a row. This is awfully exciting. He's plunged both his hands into her hair.

FREDERICK. Dirty trick, I call it.

WILLIAM. Why? She'd washed it.

FREDERICK (*bringing out a potato*). Damn it all, they're not skinned.

WILLIAM. I suppose you mean peeled.

FREDERICK. If there's anything I dislike it's potatoes in their skins.

WILLIAM. It's simply waste to peel potatoes. I never peel potatoes.

FREDERICK. Is that organization?

WILLIAM. Well, if you ask me, that's just what it is.

FREDERICK. Ever since I've been at the War Office I've heard fellows talk of organization, but I never could find anyone to tell me just what it was. It's beginning to dawn on me now.

WILLIAM (*still reading*). Well, what is it?

FREDERICK. I'm not going to tell you unless you listen.

WILLIAM (*looking up*). He's just glued his lips to hers. Well?

FREDERICK. Organization means getting someone else to do your job for you if you can, and if you can't, letting it rip. (*He replaces the potato and puts the lid on the saucepan.*)

WILLIAM. I suppose you think you're funny.

FREDERICK (*moving to the range and looking at the steak*). The steak smells as though it was almost done.

WILLIAM. Done? It's only been on about a quarter of an hour.

FREDERICK. But in a grill-room they do you steak in ten minutes.

WILLIAM. I don't care about that. You cook meat a quarter of an hour for every pound. I should have thought any fool knew that.

FREDERICK. What's that got to do with it?

WILLIAM. I bought three pounds of steak, so I'm going to cook it for three-quarters of an hour.

FREDERICK. Well, it looks to me as if it wanted eating now.

WILLIAM. That's only it's cunning. It won't be ready for ages yet. I wish you'd let me get on with my story.

FREDERICK (*moving up* C.; *puzzled*). But look here, if there were three steaks of a pound each you'd cook them a quarter of an hour each. (*He tosses the fork into the sink.*)

WILLIAM. Exactly. That's what I say. That comes to three-quarters of an hour.

FREDERICK (*above the table*). But, hang it all, it's the same quarter of an hour.

WILLIAM. You make me tired. You might just as well say that because three men can walk four miles an hour each man can walk twelve miles an hour.

FREDERICK. But that's just what I do say.

WILLIAM. Well, it's damned idiotic, that's all.

FREDERICK. No, but I mean exactly the opposite. That's what *you* say. You've got me confused now. We'll have to start all over again.

WILLIAM. I shall never finish this story if you go on like this.

FREDERICK. It's a very important matter. (*He moves to the dresser.*) Let's get a pencil and a piece of paper and work it out. (*He gets the grocery-pad and pencil off the hook.*)

(*The bell starts to ring.*)

(*He looks up at the bell.*) Quiet!

(*The bell stops.*)

(*He moves above the table.*) We must get it right. (*He sits in the chair above the* L. *end of the table and starts to work out a sum.*)

WILLIAM. For goodness' sake go and clean knives or something, and don't bother your head about things that are no concern of yours.

FREDERICK. Who's going to eat the steak?

WILLIAM. You won't if you're not careful.

FREDERICK. If I'm careful I don't think I will.

WILLIAM (*beginning to grow peevish*). Cooking has its rules like

everything else, and it's just as little use arguing about them as arguing about women.

FREDERICK. Now look here, if you cut that steak into three, would there be three pounds of steak or not?

WILLIAM. Certainly not. There'd be three steaks of one pound, and that's quite another matter.

FREDERICK. But it would be the same steak.

WILLIAM (*rising; emphatically*). It wouldn't be the same steak. It would be an entirely different steak.

FREDERICK (*rising*). Do you mean to tell me that if you had a steak of a hundred pounds you'd cook it for twenty-five hours?

WILLIAM. Yes, and if I had a steak a thousand pounds I'd cook it for ten days. (*He perches himself on the* L. *end of the table and tries to get on with his novel.*)

FREDERICK. It seems an awful waste of gas.

WILLIAM. I don't care about that, it's logic.

(VICTORIA *enters up* R. *She is dressed for outdoors.* WILLIAM *rises.*)

VICTORIA (*moving to* R. *of the table*). I really think it's too bad of you. I've been ringing the bell for the last quarter of an hour. There are two men in the house and you neither of you pay the least attention.

WILLIAM. We were having an argument.

FREDERICK. Let me put it before you, Victoria.

WILLIAM. It has nothing to do with Victoria. I'm the cook, and I won't have anyone come interfering in my kitchen.

FREDERICK. You must do something, Victoria. The steak will be absolutely uneatable.

VICTORIA. I don't care. I never eat steak.

WILLIAM. It's all you'll get for luncheon.

VICTORIA. I shan't be here for luncheon.

WILLIAM. Why not?

VICTORIA. Because—because Mr Leicester Paton has made me an offer of marriage and I have accepted it.

FREDERICK. But you've got two husbands already, Victoria.

VICTORIA. I imagine you'll both be gentlemen enough to put no obstacle in the way of my getting my freedom.

(*The bell rings.*)

FREDERICK. Hulloa, who's that?

VICTORIA. That is my solicitor.

FREDERICK. Your what?

VICTORIA. I told him to come at once. Go and open the door, Freddie, will you?

FREDERICK. What the dickens does he want?

VICTORIA. He's going to fix up my divorce.

FREDERICK (*taking off his apron*). You're not letting the grass grow under your feet.

(*He puts the apron on the chair up* R., *then exits up* R.)

WILLIAM (*taking off his apron*). This is a desperate step you're taking, Victoria. (*He hangs the apron on the hook up* L., *takes down his jacket and puts it on.*)

VICTORIA. I had to do something. You must see that it's quite impossible for a woman to live without servants. I had no-one to do me up this morning.

WILLIAM. How on earth did you manage?

VICTORIA (*sitting on the chair* R. *of the table*). I had to put on something that didn't need doing up.

WILLIAM (L. *of the table*). That seems an adequate way out of the difficulty.

VICTORIA. It so happens that the one frock that didn't need doing up was the one frock I didn't want to wear.

WILLIAM. You look ravishing in it all the same.

VICTORIA (*rather stiffly*). I'd sooner you didn't pay me compliments, Bill.

WILLIAM. Why not?

VICTORIA. Well, now that I'm engaged to Leicester Paton I don't think it's very good form.

WILLIAM. Have you quite made up your mind to divorce me?

VICTORIA. Quite.

WILLIAM (*moving to* VICTORIA). In that case, I can almost look upon you as another man's wife.

VICTORIA. What do you mean by that?

WILLIAM (*pulling* VICTORIA *to her feet*). Only that I can make love to you without feeling a thundering ass.

VICTORIA (*smiling*). I'm not going to let you make love to me.

WILLIAM. You can't prevent me from telling you that you're the loveliest thing that ever turned a poor man's head.

VICTORIA. I can close my ears.

WILLIAM (*taking her hands*). Impossible, for I shall hold your hands.

VICTORIA. I shall scream.

WILLIAM. You can't, because I shall kiss your lips. (*He kisses her.*)

VICTORIA. Oh, Bill, what a pity it is you were ever my husband. I'm sure you'd make a charming lover.

WILLIAM. I have often thought that is the better part.

VICTORIA. Take care. (*She moves down* R.) They're just coming. It would never do for my solicitor to find me in my husband's arms.

WILLIAM (*moving* L.C.). It would be outrageous.

(FREDERICK *enters up* R. *and ushers in* A. B. RAHAM, *a solicitor. There is nothing more to be said about him. He carries his hat and a brief-case*

VICTORIA. How do you do, Mr Raham? Do you know my husbands?

(FREDERICK *moves up* L.C.)

RAHAM (*putting his hat on the chair up* R.). I'm pleased to meet you, gentlemen. (*He moves to* R. *of the table and puts his brief-case on it.*) I dare say it will facilitate matters if I am told which of you is which, and which is the other.

VICTORIA (*indicating* WILLIAM). This is Major Cardew, my first husband.

(RAHAM *moves below the table to* WILLIAM *and shakes hands with him.*)

(*She indicates* FREDERICK.) And this is my second husband, Major Lowndes.

RAHAM (*moving* R. *of the table*). Ah, that makes it quite clear. (*He moves above the table to* FREDERICK *and shakes hands with him.*) Interesting coincidence—both Majors.

WILLIAM. I suppose that Mrs Lowndes has put you in possession of the facts, Mr Raham.

RAHAM. I think so. (*He draws out the chair above the* L. *end of the table and nods to* VICTORIA.)

(VICTORIA *moves above the table and sits in the chair* RAHAM *has set for her.*)

We had a long talk at my office yesterday. (*He moves to the chair* R. *of the table and sits.*)

FREDERICK (*sitting in the chair above the* R. *end of the table.*) You can quite understand that it's a position of some delicacy for Mrs Cardew.

RAHAM (*puzzled*). Mrs Cardew? Where does Mrs Cardew come in?

FREDERICK. This is Mrs Cardew.

RAHAM. Oh, I see what you mean. That, in short, is the difficulty. Is this lady Mrs Cardew or Mrs Lowndes? Well, the fact is, she has decided to be neither.

VICTORIA. I've just broken it to them.

WILLIAM (*sitting in the chair* L. *of the table*). You find us still staggering from the shock.

FREDERICK. Staggering.

RAHAM. She has determined to divorce you both. I have told her that this is not necessary, since she is obviously the wife of only one of you.

VICTORIA (*argumentatively*). In that case, what am I to the other?

RAHAM. Well, Mrs Cardew, or shall we say Lowndes? I hardly like to mention it to a lady, but if you'll excuse me saying so, you're his concubine.

WILLIAM. I rather like that, it sounds so damned Oriental.

VICTORIA (*indignantly*). I never heard of such a thing.

WILLIAM. Oh, Fatima, your face is like the full moon, and your eyes are like the eyes of a young gazelle. Come, dance to me to the sound of the lute.

VICTORIA. Well, that settles it. I shall divorce them both just to prove to everyone that they're both my husbands.

FREDERICK. I think it's just as well to take no risks.

RAHAM. Do I understand that you two gentlemen are agreeable?

WILLIAM. Speaking for myself, I am prepared to sacrifice my feelings, deep as they are, to the happiness of Victoria.

RAHAM. Very nicely and feelingly put.

VICTORIA. He always was a gentleman.

RAHAM (to FREDERICK). Now you, Major Cardew.

FREDERICK. My name is Lowndes.

RAHAM. My mistake. Of course you're Major Lowndes. I made a mental note of it when we were introduced. Cardew—camel-face. Lowndes—litigation. Pelmanism, you know.

FREDERICK. I see. It doesn't seem very effective, though.

RAHAM. Anyhow, that is neither here nor there. Will you give this lady the freedom she desires?

FREDERICK. I will. (With a puzzled look.) When did I last say those words? (He remembers.) Of course, the marriage service.

RAHAM (opening his brief-case). Well, so far so good. (He takes a sheaf of papers out of the case.) I am under the impression that when it comes to the point we shall not need to take both you gentlemen into court, but I quite agree with Mrs Lowndes-Cardew that it will save time and trouble if we get up the case against both of you in the same way. Since you will neither of you defend the case, there is no need for you to go to the expense of legal advice, so I propose to go into the whole matter with you now.

VICTORIA. You can feel quite easy about taking Mr Raham's advice. He has arranged more divorce cases than any man in England.

RAHAM. I venture to say that there are few of the best families in this country that haven't made use of my services in one way or another. Outraged husband, deceived wife, co-respondent or intervener; it's hardly likely that anyone who is anyone won't figure sooner or later in one or other of these capacities. And although I say it myself, if he's wise he comes to me. My maxim has always been—do it quickly; don't let's have a lot of fuss and bother. And, just to show you how my system works, there are ladies for whom I've got a divorce from three or four successive husbands, and never a word of scandal has sullied the purity of their fair name.

WILLIAM. You must be a very busy man.

RAHAM. I assure you, Major, I'm one of the busiest men in London.

WILLIAM. Fortunately, some marriages are happy.

RAHAM. Don't you believe it, Major Cardew. There are no happy marriages. But there are some that are tolerable.

VICTORIA. You are a pessimist, Mr Raham. I have made both my husbands ideally happy.

RAHAM. But I will come to the point. Though, perhaps, it is hardly necessary, I will point out to you gentlemen what the law of the country needs in order to free a couple who, for reasons which merely concern themselves, have decided that they prefer to part company. If a husband wishes to divorce his wife he need prove nothing but adultery, but the English law recognizes the natural polygamy of man, and when a wife desires to divorce her husband she must prove besides cruelty or desertion. Let us take these first. Do you wish the cause of offence to be cruelty *or* desertion?

VICTORIA. Personally, I should prefer desertion.

WILLIAM. Certainly. I should very much dislike to be cruel to you, Victoria.

FREDERICK. And you know I could never hurt a fly.

RAHAM. Then we will settle on desertion. I think myself it is the more gentlemanly way, and besides, it is more easily proved. The procedure is excessively simple. Mrs Cardew-Lowndes will write you a letter, which I shall dictate, asking you to return to her—the usual phrase is "to make a home for her"—and you will refuse. I propose that you should both give me your refusals now.

WILLIAM (*surprised*). Before we've had the letter?

RAHAM. Precisely. The letter which she will write, and which is read out in court, is so touching that on one occasion the husband, about to be divorced, was so moved that he immediately returned to his wife. She was very angry indeed, and so now I invariably get the refusal first.

WILLIAM. It's so difficult to write an answer to a letter that hasn't been written.

RAHAM. To meet that difficulty, I have also prepared the replies. Have you a fountain-pen?

WILLIAM. Yes. (*He takes a fountain-pen from his pocket.*)

RAHAM (*selecting two sheets of paper from the pile in front of him*). If you will kindly write to my dictation, we will settle the matter at once. (*He rises, moves below the table to* WILLIAM *and hands him one of the sheets of paper.*)

WILLIAM (*looking at the paper*). The address is—*Hotel Majestic.*

RAHAM (*moving* R. *of the table*). You will see the point later. (*He gives the other sheet to* FREDERICK.) Here is a piece for you, Major.

FREDERICK. Do we both write the same letter?

RAHAM. Certainly not. I have two letters that I generally make use of, and I propose that you should each of you write one of them. The note of one is sorrow rather than anger. The other is somewhat vituperative. You can decide among yourselves which of you had better write which.

Victoria. They both habitually swore at me, but I think Bill's language was more varied.

Raham. That settles it. (*To* Frederick.) Are you ready, Major Lowndes?

Frederick (*stretching out his hand to* William *for the pen*). Fire away.

(William *passes the pen to* Frederick.)

Raham (*dictating*). My dear Victoria, I have given your letter anxious consideration. (*He moves up* c.) If I thought there was any hope of our making a greater success of married life in the future than we have in the past I should be the first to suggest that we should make one more attempt.

(Frederick *writes furiously.*)

William. Very touching.

Raham (*continuing*). But I have regretfully come to the conclusion that to return to you would only be to cause a recurrence of the unhappy life from which I know that you have suffered no less than I. (*He moves* r.) I am bound therefore definitely to refuse your request. I do not propose under any circumstances to return to you. (*He moves to* r. *of the table.*) Yours sincerely. Now sign your full name.

(Frederick *signs the letter.*)

Victoria (*taking the letter*). A very nice letter, Freddie. (*She reads the letter.*) I shall always think pleasantly of you. (*She passes the letter to* Raham.)

Frederick. I have my points. (*He returns the pen to* William.)

Raham. Now, Major Cardew, are you ready? (*He puts the letter with his papers.*)

William. Quite.

Raham (*dictating*). My dear Victoria, I am in receipt of your letter asking me to return to you. Our life together has been a hell upon earth, and I have long realized that our marriage was a tragic mistake. You have sickened me with scenes and tortured me with jealousy. (*He moves below the table to* l. *of it.*) If you have tried to make me happy you have succeeded singularly ill. I trust that I shall never see you again, and nothing in the world will induce me ever to resume a life which I can only describe as a miserable degradation.

William (*writing furiously*). Thick, eh?

Raham. Now the crowning touch. Mark the irony of the polite ending: I beg to remain yours most sincerely. Now sign your name.

(William *signs the letter.*)

William. I've signed it. (*He puts his pen in his pocket.*)

Raham (*taking the letter from* William). Then that is settled,

(*He moves to* R. *of the table and puts the letter with his papers.*) Now we only have to go into court, apply for a decree for restitution of conjugal rights, and six months later bring an action for divorce.

VICTORIA. Six months later! But when shall I be free, then?

RAHAM. In about a year.

VICTORIA. Oh, but that won't do at all. I must have my freedom by—well, before the racing season ends at all events.

RAHAM. As soon as that?

VICTORIA. *The Derby*, if possible. Certainly by the *Two Thousand Guineas*.

RAHAM (*shrugging his shoulders*). In that case the only thing is cruelty.

VICTORIA. It can't be helped. They'll have to be cruel.

FREDERICK. I don't like the idea, Victoria.

VICTORIA. Try and be a little unselfish for once, darling.

WILLIAM. I could never strike a woman.

VICTORIA. If I don't mind I don't see why you should.

RAHAM. Cruelty has its advantages. If it's properly witnessed it has a convincing air which desertion never has.

VICTORIA. My mother will swear to anything.

RAHAM. Servants are better. The judges are often unduly suspicious of the mother-in-law's testimony. Of course, one has to be careful. Once, I remember, on my instructions the guilty husband hit the lady I was acting for in the jaw, which unfortunately knocked out her false teeth. The gentleman she had arranged to marry happened to be present and he was so startled that he took the night train for the Continent and has never been heard of since.

WILLIAM. I'm happy to say that Victoria's teeth are all her own.

RAHAM. On another occasion I recommended a gentleman to take a stick and give his wife a few strokes with it. I don't know if he got excited or what, but he gave her a regular hiding.

VICTORIA. How awful!

RAHAM. It was indeed, for she threw her arms round his neck, and, saying she adored him, refused to have anything more to do with the divorce. She was going to marry a colonel in the army, and he was most offensive to me about it. I had to tell him that if he didn't leave my office I would send for the police.

VICTORIA. You're dreadfully discouraging.

RAHAM. Oh, I merely tell you that to show you what may happen. But I have devised my own system and I have never known it fail. I always arrange for three definite acts of cruelty. First at the dinner-table. Now, please listen to me carefully, gentlemen, and follow my instructions to the letter. When you have tasted your soup you throw down the spoon with a clatter and say, "Good Lord, this soup is uneatable. Can't you get a decent cook?" You, madam, will answer, "I do my best, darling."

Upon which you, crying with a loud voice, "Take that, you damned fool," throw the plate straight at her. With a little ingenuity the lady can dodge the plate, and the only damage is done to the tablecloth.

VICTORIA. I like that.

RAHAM. The second act is a little more violent. (*To* WILLIAM.) I suppose you have a revolver?

WILLIAM. At all events, I can get one.

RAHAM. Having carefully removed the cartridges, you ring the bell for the servant, and just as she opens the door, you point it at the lady and say, "You lying devil, I'll kill you." Then you, madam, give a loud shriek, and cry to the maid, "Oh, save me, save me."

VICTORIA. I shall love doing that. So dramatic.

RAHAM. I think it's effective. When the servant tells her story in court it is very seldom that an audible thrill does not pass over the audience. They describe it in the papers as: "Sensation."

VICTORIA (*practising*). Oh, save me. Save me.

RAHAM. Now we come to physical as opposed to moral cruelty. It's as well to have two witnesses to this. The gentleman takes the lady by the throat, at the same time hissing malevolently, "I'll throttle you if I swing for it, by God". It's very important to leave a bruise so that the doctor, who should be sent for immediately, can swear to it.

VICTORIA. I don't like that part so much.

(FREDERICK *rises*.)

RAHAM. Believe me, it's no more unpleasant than having a tooth stopped. Now if one of you gentlemen would just go up to the lady we'll practise that. I set great store on this particular point, and it's important that there should be no mistake. Major Cardew, would you mind obliging?

WILLIAM (*rising*). Not at all.

VICTORIA (*rising*). Be careful, Bill.

WILLIAM (*leading* VICTORIA *below the table*). Do I take her with both hands or only one?

(FREDERICK *sits on the chair above the* L. *end of the table*.)

RAHAM. Only one.

(WILLIAM *seizes* VICTORIA *by the throat*.)

That's right. (*To* VICTORIA.) If he doesn't press hard enough kick him on the shins.

WILLIAM. If you do, Victoria, I swear I'll kick you back.

RAHAM. That's the spirit. You can't make a bruise without a little violence. Now hiss.

VICTORIA. I'm choking.

RAHAM. Hiss, hiss.

WILLIAM. "I'll throttle you if I swing for it, by God." (*He releases* VICTORIA.)

RAHAM. Splendid! A real artist. You're as good as divorced already.

VICTORIA (*sitting* L. *of the table*). He did say it well, didn't he? It really made my blood turn cold.

(WILLIAM *moves to the dresser.*)

FREDERICK (*eagerly*). Do you want me to do it, too?

RAHAM. Now you've seen the idea I think it'll do if you just practise it once or twice with Major Cardew.

FREDERICK (*disappointed*). Oh, all right.

(WILLIAM *takes a cigarette from the packet on the dresser, and lights it.*)

RAHAM. Now we come to a point trivial enough in itself, but essential in order to satisfy the requirements of our English law. Adultery.

WILLIAM. That, I think, you can safely leave to us.

RAHAM. By no means. I think that would be most dangerous.

WILLIAM. Hang it all, man, human nature can surely be trusted there.

RAHAM. We are not dealing with human nature, we are dealing with law.

WILLIAM. Law be blowed. With the price of a supper in my pocket and an engaging manner I am prepared to supply you with all the evidence you want.

RAHAM. I am shocked and horrified by your suggestion. Do you expect a man in my position to connive at immorality?

WILLIAM. Immorality. Well, there must be—shall we say, a *soupçon* of it—under the painful circumstances.

RAHAM. Not at all. I always arrange this part of the proceedings with the most scrupulous regard to propriety. And before we go any further I should like to inform you that unless you are prepared to put out of your mind anything that is suggestive of indecent behaviour I shall decline to have anything more to do with the case.

VICTORIA. I think you must have a nasty mind, Bill.

WILLIAM. But, my dear Victoria, I only wanted to make things easy for you. I apologize. I put myself in your hands, Mr Raham.

RAHAM. Then please listen to me. I will engage a suite of rooms for you at the *Hotel Majestic*. You will remember it was from there you wrote the letter in which you declined to return to your wife. The judge never fails to remark on the coincidence. On a date to be settled hereafter you will come to my office, where you will meet a lady.

WILLIAM. Do you mean to say you provide her, too?

RAHAM. Certainly.

FREDERICK. What's she like?

RAHAM. A most respectable person. I have employed her in these cases for many years.

WILLIAM. It sounds as though she made a business of it.

RAHAM. She does.

FREDERICK. What!

RAHAM. Yes, she had the idea—a most ingenious one to my mind—that in these days of specialized professions there was great need for someone to undertake the duties of intervener. That is the name by which the lady is known, adultery with whom is the motive for divorce. She has been employed by the best legal firms in London, and she has figured in practically all the fashionable divorces of the last fifteen years.

WILLIAM. You amaze me.

RAHAM. I have felt it my duty to give her all the work I can on account of a paralyzed father, whom she supports entirely by her exertions.

VICTORIA. Not an unpleasant existence, I should imagine.

RAHAM. If you knew her you would realize that no thought of that has ever entered her mind. A most unselfish, noble-minded woman.

WILLIAM. Does she make money by it?

RAHAM. Sufficient for her simple needs. She only charges twenty guineas for her services.

WILLIAM. I'm sure I could get it done for less.

RAHAM. Not by a woman of any refinement.

WILLIAM. Well, well, with most of us it's only once in a lifetime.

RAHAM. I will proceed. You will fetch this lady at my office, and you will drive with her to the *Hotel Majestic*, where you will register as Major and Mrs Cardew. You will be shown into the suite of rooms which I shall engage for you, and supper will be served in the sitting-room. You will partake of this, and you will drink champagne.

WILLIAM. I should like to choose the brand myself.

RAHAM (*magnanimously*). I have no objection to that.

WILLIAM. Thanks.

RAHAM. Then you will play cards. Miss Montmorency is a wonderful card-player. She not only has an unparalleled knowledge of all games for two, but she can do a great number of tricks. In this way you will find the night pass without tediousness, and in the morning you will ring for breakfast.

FREDERICK. I'm not sure if I should have much appetite for it.

RAHAM. I never mind my clients having brandy and soda instead. It looks well in the waiter's evidence. And after having paid your bill, you will take Miss Montmorency in a taxi-cab and deposit her at my office.

WILLIAM. It sounds a devil of a beano.

FREDERICK. I should like to see her first.

RAHAM. That is perfectly easy. I know that ladies in these

cases often like to see the intervener themselves. Ladies are sometimes very suspicious, and even though they're getting rid of their
husbands, they don't want them to—well, run any risks; and so
I took the liberty of bringing Miss Montmorency with me. She
is waiting in the taxi at the door, and if you like I will go and
fetch her.

FREDERICK (rising). No. (He moves up R.) I'll go along and bring
her down.

VICTORIA. Is she the sort of person I should like to meet, Mr
Raham?

RAHAM. Oh, a perfect lady. She comes from one of the best
families in Shropshire.

VICTORIA. Do fetch her, Freddie.

(FREDERICK exits up R.)

Now I come to think of it, I should like to see her. Men are so
weak, and I shall be easier in my mind if I can be sure that these
poor boys won't be led astray.

(WILLIAM moves the chair from above the dresser and puts it C. above the
table.)

WILLIAM (to RAHAM). Do you mean to say that with this evidence you will be able to get a divorce?

RAHAM (easing down R.). Not a doubt of it. I've got hundreds.

WILLIAM. I am only a soldier, and I dare say you will not be
surprised if I am mentally deficient.

RAHAM. Not at all. Not at all.

(FREDERICK enters up R. He is pale and dishevelled. He staggers into
the room like a man who has been exposed to a tremendous shock.)

FREDERICK (gasping). Brandy! Brandy! (He crosses to the dresser.

WILLIAM. What's the matter?

FREDERICK. Brandy! (He fills almost half a glass with brandy from
the decanter on the dresser, and swallows it neat.)

MISS MONTMORENCY (off, up R.). Is this the way?

RAHAM (calling). Come straight in, Miss Montmorency.

(MISS MONTMORENCY enters up R. She is a spinster of uncertain age.
She might be fifty-five. She looks rather like a hard-boiled egg, but there
is in her gestures a languid grace. She speaks with a slight drawl, pro-
nouncing her words with refinement, and her manner is a mixture of
affability and condescension. She might be a governess in a very good
family in the suburbs. Her respectability is portentous. She carries a
handbag. FREDERICK replaces the glass on the dresser and breaks down
L.)

MISS MONTMORENCY (looking around). But this is the kitchen.

E

(WILLIAM *takes a long look at* MISS MONTMORENCY *then moves to the dresser and pours out a brandy for himself. His hand shakes so violently that the neck of the decanter rattles against the glass. He swallows the drink neat, then replaces the glass on the dresser.*)

VICTORIA (*rising*). I'm afraid it's the only room in the house that's habitable at the moment.

MISS MONTMORENCY. To the practised observer the signs of domestic infelicity jump to the eye, as the French say.

RAHAM (*introducing*). Miss Montmorency—Mrs Frederick Lowndes.

MISS MONTMORENCY (*graciously*). I'm charmed to make your acquaintance. The injured wife, I presume?

VICTORIA. Er—yes.

MISS MONTMORENCY. So sad. So sad. I'm afraid the war is responsible for the rupture of many happy marriages. I'm booked up for weeks ahead. So sad. So sad.

VICTORIA (*indicating the chair* WILLIAM *has set up* C.). Do sit down, won't you?

MISS MONTMORENCY (*moving above the table*). Thank you. (*She sits.*) Do you mind if I get out my notebook? I like to get everything perfectly clear, and my memory isn't what it was. (*She takes a notebook and pencil from her handbag.*)

VICTORIA (*sitting* L. *of the table*). Of course.

(RAHAM *sits* R. *of the table.*)

MISS MONTMORENCY. And now, which of these gentlemen is the erring husband?

VICTORIA. Well, they both are.

MISS MONTMORENCY. Oh, really. And which are you going to marry after you've got your divorce?

VICTORIA. Neither.

MISS MONTMORENCY. This is a very peculiar case, Mr Raham. When I saw these two gentlemen I naturally concluded that one of them was the husband Mrs Frederick Lowndes was discarding and the other the husband she was acquiring. The eternal triangle, you know.

WILLIAM. In this case the triangle is four-sided.

MISS MONTMORENCY. Oh, how very peculiar.

RAHAM. We see a lot of strange things in our business, Miss Montmorency.

MISS MONTMORENCY. To whom do you say it, as the French say.

VICTORIA. I don't want you to think that I've been at all light or careless, but the fact is, through no fault of my own, they're both my husbands.

MISS MONTMORENCY (*taking it as a matter of course*). Oh really. How very interesting. And which are you divorcing?

VICTORIA. I'm divorcing them both.

Miss Montmorency. Oh, I see. Very sad. Very sad.

William (*moving and sitting* l. *of* Miss Montmorency). We're taking as cheerful a view of it as we can.

Miss Montmorency. Ah, yes, that's what I say to my clients. Courage. Courage.

Frederick (*with a start*). When? (*He moves and sits* r. *of* Miss Montmorency.)

Victoria. Be quiet, Freddie.

Miss Montmorency. I think I ought to tell you at once that I shouldn't like to misconduct myself—I use the technical expression—with both these gentlemen.

Raham. Oh, Miss Montmorency, a woman of your experience isn't going to strain at a gnat.

Miss Montmorency. No, but I shouldn't like to swallow a camel.

Raham. We shall be generous, Miss Montmorency.

Miss Montmorency. I have to think of my self-respect. One gentleman is business, but two would be debauchery.

Raham. Mrs Lowndes is anxious to put this matter through as quickly as possible.

Miss Montmorency. I dare say my friend Mrs Onslow Jervis would oblige if I asked her as a personal favour.

Victoria. Are you sure she can be trusted?

Miss Montmorency. Oh, she's a perfect lady and most respectable. She's the widow of a clergyman, and she has two sons in the army. They've done so well in the war.

Raham. Unless we can get Miss Montmorency to reconsider her decision I'm afraid we shall have to put up with Mrs Onslow Jervis.

Miss Montmorency. I am adamant, Mr Raham. Adamant.

Frederick. I'm all for Mrs Onslow Jervis personally.

Miss Montmorency (*to* William). Then you fall to me, Major ... I didn't catch your name.

William. Cardew.

Miss Montmorency. I hope you play cards.

William. Sometimes.

Miss Montmorency. I'm a great card-player. Piquet, écarté, cribbage, double rummy, baccarat, bezique, I don't mind what I play. It's such a relief to find a gentleman who's fond of cards.

William. Otherwise I dare say the night seems rather long.

Miss Montmorency. Oh, not to me, you know. I'm such a student of human nature. But my gentlemen begin to grow a little restless when I've talked to them for six or seven hours.

William. I can hardly believe it.

Miss Montmorency. One gentleman actually said he wanted to go to bed, but, of course, I told him that would never do.

Victoria. Forgive my asking—you know what men are—do they never attempt to take any liberties with you?

Miss Montmorency. Oh no. If you're a lady you can always keep a man in his place. And Mr Raham only takes the very best sort of divorces. The only unpleasantness I've ever had was with a gentleman sent to me by a firm of solicitors in a cathedral city.

William. I can assure you, Miss Montmorency, that you need have no fear that I shall take advantage of your delicate position.

Miss Montmorency. Of course, you will divest yourself of none of your raiment.

William. On the contrary, I propose to put on an extra suit of clothes.

Miss Montmorency. Oh, Mr Raham, please don't forget that I only drink Pommery. In the Twickenham divorce they sent up Pol Roger, and Pol Roger always gives me indigestion.

Raham. I've made a note of it.

Miss Montmorency. Nineteen-o-six. (*To* William.) I'm sure we shall have a delightful night. I can see that we have much in common.

(Raham *collects his papers together and puts them in the brief-case.*)

William. It's too good of you to say so.

Miss Montmorency (*to* Frederick). And I know you'll like Mrs Onslow Jervis. A perfect lady. She has such charm of manners. So much ease. You can see that she did a lot of entertaining when her husband was Vicar of Clacton. They have a very nice class of people at Clacton.

Frederick. I shall be charmed to meet her.

Miss Montmorency. I don't know what Mr Raham would say to our sharing a suite. We could play bridge. She's a very fine bridge-player, and we only play threepence a hundred, because in her position she can hardly gamble, can she?

Raham. I always like to oblige you, Miss Montmorency, but I hardly think that arrangement would do. You know how fussy the judges are. We might hit upon one of them who saw nothing in it.

Miss Montmorency (*replacing her notebook and pencil in her handbag*). Oh, well, let us take no risks. (*She rises.*) Business is business.

(Raham, Frederick *and* William *rise.*)

It must be you and me alone then, Major Cardew. You will let me know in good time when you fix the fatal night.

(William *puts his chair against the wall above the dresser, then eases up* L. Frederick *puts his chair up* L.C. *near the sink, then eases down* R.)

I'm very booked up just now.

Raham (*picking up his brief-case*). Of course, we will do everything to suit your convenience, Miss Montmorency. And now, Mrs Lowndes, since we have settled everything, I think Miss Montmorency and I will go. (*He gets his hat from up* R.)

VICTORIA (*rising*). I can't think of anything else.

MISS MONTMORENCY. Good-bye, then. (*To* WILLIAM.) I'm not going to say good-bye to you, but *au revoir*.

WILLIAM. Believe me, I look forward to our next meeting.

RAHAM. Good morning, Mrs Lowndes. Good morning. (*He moves towards the door up* C.) Shall we go out this way?

(WILLIAM *moves to the door up* C. *and opens it.*)

MISS MONTMORENCY (*just a little taken back*). The area steps? Oh, very well. It's so quaint and old-fashioned. I always think a lady if she is a lady can do anything.

(*She gives a gracious bow and exits up* C. *followed by* RAHAM.)

WILLIAM (*closing the door*). This is a bit of all right that you've let us in for, Victoria.

VICTORIA (*moving below the table*). Well, darling, it's the only thing I've ever asked you to do for me in all my life, so you needn't complain.

WILLIAM (*moving* L. *of the table*). I will bear it like a martyr.

VICTORIA. Now, the only thing left is for me to bid you good-bye.

FREDERICK (*moving* R. *of the table*). Already?

VICTORIA. You must understand that under the circumstances it wouldn't be quite nice for me to stay here. Besides, without servants, it's beastly uncomfortable.

WILLIAM. Won't you even stay to luncheon?

VICTORIA. I don't think I will, thanks. I think I shall get a better one at mother's.

FREDERICK. Oh, are you going there?

VICTORIA. Where else do you expect a woman to go in a crisis like this?

WILLIAM. I should think the steak was about done, Freddie.

FREDERICK. Oh, I'd give it another hour or two to make sure.

VICTORIA. Of course, I realize that it's a painful moment for both of you, but as you say, we shan't make it any easier by dragging it out.

WILLIAM. True.

VICTORIA. Good-bye, Bill. I forgive you everything, and I hope we shall always be good friends.

WILLIAM (*moving to* L. *of* VICTORIA). Good-bye, Victoria. I hope this will not be by any means your last marriage.

VICTORIA. When everything is settled you must come and dine with us. I'm sure you'll find that Leicester has the best wines and cigars that money can buy. (*She offers him an indifferent cheek.*)

WILLIAM (*kissing* VICTORIA's *left cheek.*) Good-bye.

VICTORIA. And now, Freddie, it's your turn. Now that there's nothing more between us you might give me back that pin I gave you.

FREDERICK (*taking the pin out of his tie*). Here you are.

VICTORIA (*taking the pin*). And there was a cigarette-case. (*She takes the case out of* FREDERICK's *outside left jacket pocket.*)

FREDERICK. Take it.

VICTORIA (*putting the pin and case in her handbag*). They say jewellery has gone up tremendously in value since the war. I shall give Leicester a cigarette-case as a wedding present.

WILLIAM. You always do, Victoria.

VICTORIA. Men like it. Good-bye, Freddie dear. I shall always have a pleasant recollection of you. (*She offers him her right cheek.*)

FREDERICK. Good-bye, Victoria. (*He kisses her right cheek.*)

WILLIAM (*moving to the door up* C.). Would you like a taxi? (*He opens the door.*)

VICTORIA (*moving to the door up* C.). No, thanks. I think the exercise will do me good.

(*She exits up* C. *and is seen tripping up the area steps.*)

FREDERICK (*easing up* R.). A wonderful woman.

WILLIAM (*closing the door*). I shall never regret having married her. Now let's have lunch. (*He moves to the dresser, gets the dish from the second shelf and crosses below the table to the range.*)

FREDERICK (*moving to the dresser and getting two plates*). I wish I looked forward to it as much as you do. (*He moves to the table and puts the plates on it.*)

WILLIAM. Dear old man, has this affecting scene taken away your appetite?

FREDERICK (*setting out knives and forks from the cutlery basket*). It's not the appetite I'm doubtful about. It's the steak. (*He takes the cutlery basket to the dresser and returns to the table with the cruet.*)

WILLIAM (*picking up the fish-slice*). Oh, don't you worry yourself about that. I'll just dish up. (*He tries to get the steak out of the frying-pan.*) Come out, you great fat devil. It won't come out.

FREDERICK. That's your trouble.

WILLIAM (*bringing the frying-pan to the table*). Oh, well, we can eat it just as well out of the frying-pan. Shall I carve it?

FREDERICK (*sitting* L. *of the table*). Please.

(WILLIAM, R. *of the table, takes a knife and starts to cut the steak. It won't cut. He applies force. The steak resists stealthily. A little surprised,* WILLIAM *puts somewhat more strength into it. He makes no impression. He begins to grow vexed. He starts to struggle. He sets his teeth. It is all in vain. The sweat pours from his brow.* FREDERICK *watches him in gloomy silence. At last, in a passion,* WILLIAM *throws down the knife.*)

WILLIAM (*furiously*). Why don't you say something, you fool?

FREDERICK (*gently*). Shall I go and fetch my little hatchet?

WILLIAM (*attacking the steak again angrily with the knife*). I know my theory's right. If you cook a pound of meat a quarter of an hour you must cook three pounds of meat three quarters of an hour.

(CLARENCE, *an errand boy, carrying a large picnic basket, is seen coming down the area steps. He knocks at the door up* C.)

FREDERICK (*rising*). Hulloa, who's this? (*He moves to the door up* C. *and opens it.*) What can I do for you, my son?

CLARENCE. Does Mrs Frederick Lowndes live here?

FREDERICK. In a manner of speaking.

CLARENCE (*indicating the basket*). From the *Ritz Hotel*.

FREDERICK. What's that? Walk right in, my boy. Put it on the table.

(CLARENCE *enters and puts the basket on the table.*)

WILLIAM (*looking at the label*). With Mr Leicester Paton's compliments.

FREDERICK (L. *of* CLARENCE). It's luncheon. (*He opens the basket.*)

CLARENCE (*banging the lid down on to* FREDERICK's *hand*). I was told to give the basket to the lady personally.

FREDERICK (*wincing and pushing the lid open again*). That's all right, my boy.

(WILLIAM *and* FREDERICK *both reach into the basket.*)

CLARENCE (*banging the lid shut on to their hands*). If the lady's not here I'm to take it back again.

WILLIAM (*promptly*). She's just coming downstairs. (*He moves up* R. *and calls.*) Victoria, my darling, that kind Mr Leicester Paton has sent you a little light refreshment from the *Ritz*.

FREDERICK (*taking a coin from his pocket*). There's half-a-crown for you, my lad. (*He gives* CLARENCE *the coin.*) Now, you hop it quick.

CLARENCE (*moving to the door up* C.). Thank you, sir.

(*He exits up* C.)

FREDERICK. Now you can eat the steak if you like. I'm going to eat Victoria's luncheon.

WILLIAM. It's a damned unscrupulous thing to do. I'll join you.

(*They hurriedly begin to unpack the basket.*)

FREDERICK (*taking off a cover*). What's here? *Chicken en casserole?*

WILLIAM. That's all right. Here, give me that bottle and see me open it. (*He takes out a bottle of champagne.*)

FREDERICK. *Pâté de foie gras.* Good. *Caviare?* No—smoked salmon. Stout fellow, Mr Leicester Paton.

WILLIAM. Don't stand there staring at it. Get it out.

FREDERICK (*moving to the dresser*). This is a regular beano. (*He gets two glasses and puts them on the table.*)

WILLIAM (*starting to open the bottle of champagne*). I'm beginning to think the wangler won the war after all.

FREDERICK (*unpacking the rest of the basket*). *Mousse au jambon.* He's got some idea of Victoria's appetite.

WILLIAM. My dear fellow, love is always blind.

FREDERICK. Thank God for it, that's all I say. How's that cork going?

WILLIAM. Half a mo. It's just coming.

FREDERICK. This is what I call a nice little snack. Dear Victoria, she was a good sort.

WILLIAM. In her way.

FREDERICK. But give me *pâté de foie gras.*

WILLIAM (*getting the bottle opened*). Pop. Hand over your glass.

FREDERICK (*holding the glasses out for* WILLIAM). Here you are. I'm as hungry as a trooper.

WILLIAM (*filling both glasses*). Before we start, I want you to drink a toast. (*He takes one of the glasses from* FREDERICK.)

FREDERICK. I'll drink anything.

WILLIAM (*holding up his glass*). Victoria's third husband.

FREDERICK (*holding up his glass*). God help him!

They drain their glasses as—

the CURTAIN *falls.*

FURNITURE AND PROPERTY PLOT

ACT I

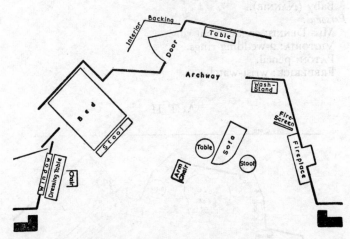

On stage:

Bed. *On it:* mattress, bolster, bedspread, 2 pillows.

Stool (*at end of bed*). *On it:* MISS DENNIS's handbag.

Dressing-table. *On it:* hand-mirror, powder-bowl, clothes-brush, hair-brush, comb, scent-spray, table lamp, cigarette box with cigarettes, bottle of perfume.

Chair (*at dressing-table*).

Console table. *On it:* vase of flowers, photographs of WILLIAM and FREDERICK in a double frame.

Washstand. *On it:* jug and bowl, vase of flowers.

Armchair. *On it:* cushion.

Table (L.C.). *On it:* manicurist's case, ashtray, cigarette box.

Stool (L.). *On it:* small towel, nail varnish, nail file, cotton-wool, orange-sticks.

Small sofa. *On it:* cushions.

On mantelpiece: clock, ornament, framed photographs, ashtray, matches.

Over mantelpiece: mirror, electric-candle wall-brackets.

Fire-screen (*above fireplace*).

Brass fender.

Fire-irons.

Hearthrug.

Pendant light (*over bed*).

Carpet on floor.

Pictures on walls.
Bell-push on wall R. of door.
Drapes over bed.
Drapes at alcove arch.
Curtains at window.
Off stage:
Baby (NANNIE).
Personal:
MISS DENNIS: engagement ring.
VICTORIA: 2 wedding rings.
PATON: pencil.
FREDERICK: wrist-watch.

ACT II

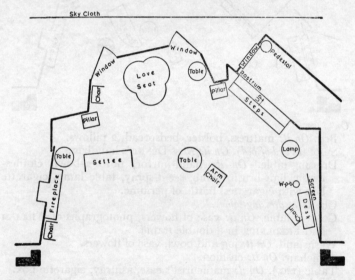

On stage:
Small chair (*down* R.).
Table (*above fireplace*). *On it:* Chinese vase.
Settee. *On it:* cushion, rug, newspaper.
Small chair (R. *of bay*).
Love-seat. *On it:* cushion. *Under the cushion:* BILL's shoes.
Table (L. *of bay*). *On it:* gramophone.
Armchair (C.). *On it:* cushion.
Table (C.). *On it:* ashtray.
Desk. *On it:* blotter, inkstand, pencils, table lamp.
    In desk drawer: 2 small pieces of paper.
Waste-paper basket (*above desk*).

Chair (*at desk*).
Screen (*behind desk*).
Standard lamp.
Pedestal (*in alcove*). *On it:* vase of feather palm or grasses.
On mantelpiece: clock, pair of candlesticks, vase of flowers, small
    mirror.
Over mantelpiece: mirror, candle-lamp wall-brackets.
Coal scuttle.
Fire-irons.
Brass fender.
Pictures, fans, etc. (*on walls*).
Carpet on floor.
Carpet in alcove and on alcove steps.
Net curtains at windows.
Drapes at arch.
Electric pendant.
Off stage:
    Box of chocolates (VICTORIA).
    Slip of paper (TAYLOR).
Personal:
    WILLIAM: matches.
    MRS POGSON: handbag.

ACT III

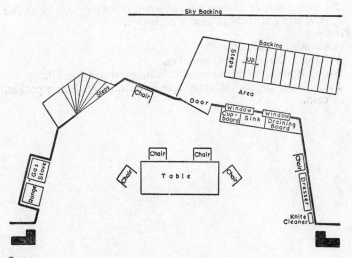

On stage:
    Dresser. *On main shelf:* cheese-dish, decanter with brandy,
    3 tumblers, packet of cigarettes, matches, ashtray, entree-
    dish, cutlery-basket with cutlery.

On downstage end of main shelf: knife-cleaner.
On 1st shelf: 6 dinner plates, cruet.
On 2nd shelf: 2 entree dishes, 1 large dish.
On top shelf: 2 tankards, coffee percolator, **tea-caddy.**
In drawer: tablecloth.
On hook downstage: rolling-pin.
On hook upstage: grocery pad and pencil.
Sink.
Draining board. *On it:* dirty crockery and saucepans.
On shelf under draining board: 2 brass hot-water cans.
Hanging over draining board: shopping bag.
Cupboard (R. *of sink*). *In it:* VICTORIA's shoes, polisher.
Table. *On it:* novel.
6 chairs.
On wall R.: roller towel, bell, indicator board.
Kitchen range. *On it:* frying pan with steak, fish-slice.
Gas-stove. *On it:* saucepan with unpeeled potatoes, kettle.
On mantelpiece: clock, household tins, teapot, copper kettle.
Hanging over stove: teacloths.
Linoleum on floor.
Set:
WILLIAM's jacket on hook up L.
Off *stage:*
Scuttle of coal (FREDERICK).
Brief-case. *In it:* papers (RAHAM).
Picnic basket. *In it: chicken en casserole,* champagne, *pâté de foie gras,* smoked salmon, *mousse au jambon.*
Personal:
VICTORIA: handbag.
WILLIAM: fountain-pen, matches.
MISS MONTMORENCY: handbag. *In it:* notebook, pencil.
FREDERICK: tiepin, cigarette-case in outside left jacket pocket, coin.